AF602050

Sentiment Analysis for Pharma Marketers

Sentiment Analysis for Pharma Marketers

Subba Rao Chaganti

™ **PharmaMed Press**

An imprint of BSP Books Pvt. Ltd.
4-4-309/316, Giriraj Lane,
Sultan Bazar, Hyderabad - 500 095.

Sentiment Analysis for Pharma Marketers
by Subba Rao Chaganti

© 2025, *by Author,* All rights reserved.

No part of this book or parts thereof may be reproduced, stored in a retrieval system or transmitted in any language or by any means, electronic, mechanical, photocopying, recording or otherwise without the prior written permission of the publishers.

Published by

PharmaMed Press™
An imprint of BSP Books Pvt. Ltd.
4-4-309/316, Giriraj Lane, Sultan Bazar, Hyderabad - 500 095.
Phone: 040-23445688, 23445600; Fax: 91+40-23445611
E-mail: info@pharmamedpress.com
www.pharmamedpress.com/pharmamedpress.net

ISBN: 978-93-48734-16-7 (Hardback)

DISCLAIMER

The information contained in this book is for informational purposes only and is not intended to be a substitute for professional medical advice, diagnosis, or treatment. Always seek the advice of your physician or other qualified healthcare provider with any questions you may have regarding a medical condition or treatment.

The publisher and author do not assume and hereby disclaim any liability for any loss, damage, or injury caused by any errors or omissions in this book or for any misuse of the information contained herein.

Examples and Case Studies:

The examples and case studies presented in this book are for illustrative purposes only and may not represent all situations.

External Resources:

While this book references external resources and tools, the publisher and author do not endorse or recommend specific products or services. You should research to determine whether external resources suit your specific needs.

PREFACE

The pharmaceutical industry's landscape is undergoing a seismic shift. Patients are no longer passive recipients of medications. They are empowered by information and actively involved in healthcare decisions, and their voices are louder than ever. In this dynamic environment, listening and understanding patient needs and concerns is no longer a luxury; it's an imperative.

This book, *Sentiment Analysis for Pharma Marketers*, is your guide to harnessing the power of sentiment analysis in this new era of patient-centricity. We'll delve into the world of big data and explore how sophisticated text analysis techniques can unlock a treasure trove of patient insights hidden within online conversations, social media posts, and reviews.

Analyzing this data allows us to move beyond basic sentiment categorization and better understand patient experiences. We'll explore techniques that reveal positive or negative sentiments and the "why" behind those opinions. We'll discover patients' anxieties about side effects, frustrations with medication regimens, and real-world experiences with treatment efficacy.

These insights are gold for the pharmaceutical industry. They inform product development efforts, allowing companies to focus on medications that address patient needs. They empower data-driven marketing strategies, ensuring patients receive clear, targeted communication that resonates with their concerns. Ultimatley, they foster stronger patient relationships built on trust and transparency.

This book is not just about theory; it's about practical application. We'll explore real-world examples of how sentiment analysis is used in the pharmaceutical industry, showcasing its transformative potential. We'll also delve into the future of sentiment analysis, exploring how AI and data science advancements will further revolutionize pharmaceutical companies' communication with patients.

Whether you are a brand manager, a market researcher, a data scientist, or simply someone with a vested interest in the future of healthcare, this book is for you. Here, you'll gain the knowledge and tools to unlock the power of patient voices and contribute to a future where medications are developed with, not just for, patients.

Let's embark on this journey of discovery together.

-Author

ACKNOWLEDGMENTS

Writing this book has been a rewarding journey, and I could not have completed it without the support and guidance of many incredible people.

First and foremost, I express my deepest gratitude to Mr. Anil Shah of PharmaMed Press, whose expertise, encouragement, and feedback were invaluable throughout the writing process. I am also grateful to Mr. Nikunjesh Shah of PharmaMed Press for his enthusiastic support in this project and for making the digital editions of this book available. A special thanks to Mr. Naresh Davergave and his design team at PharmaMed Press for making this book reader-friendly with their creative design.

My heartfelt gratitude goes to my wife, Mahalakshmi. Your unwavering support, patience, and understanding during the long hours of writing were a constant source of strength. To my children and their spouses, Srinivasa Phanindra, Geetha, Lavanya, Aditya, Sowmya, and Chaitanya, thank you for your love and encouragement. Our family's joy inspires me every day. And to my precious grandchildren, Aditi, Eesha, Surya, and Shriya, your laughter and curiosity remind me of the importance of a healthy future for all.

Finally, a big thank you to the countless patients, healthcare professionals, pharma marketers, and industry leaders who have shared their experiences and insights over the years. Your stories and perspectives have shaped my understanding of the healthcare landscape and fueled my passion for creating a more patient-centric future.

CONTENTS

PROLOGUE: THE SILENT UPRISING

The sterile silence of the hospital room was broken only by the rhythmic beeping of the heart monitor. Sarah stared at the ceiling, a dull ache throbbing in her temple. The medication she'd been prescribed for her chronic illness had finally arrived—a small victory after weeks of battling insurance companies and pharmacy delays. But a new anxiety gnawed at her.

Would it work? The online reviews were mixed—some had glowing testimonials, and others told harrowing tales of side effects. Sarah needed to decide whether to trust glossy brochures or the voices of real people like her.

Frustrated, she reached for her phone, her thumb hovering over the social media app. Maybe there were others out there who understood. Tapping the search bar, she typed in the name of the medication, a silent plea for connection echoing in the digital void.

A similar scene was unfolding across the globe in countless living rooms, hospital beds, and doctors' offices. Armed with smartphones and fueled by a desire to be heard, patients shared their experiences online. Frustrations with medications, anxieties about side effects, and triumphs over illness—a symphony of voices rising from the digital ether.

Once whispered in the dark corners of the internet, these online conversations were coalescing into a chorus that could no longer be ignored. They were an uprising of patients, a demand for transparency, and a call for medications that truly addressed their needs.

However, in pharmaceutical companies' boardrooms, the silence remained largely unbroken. Traditional market research methods, such as surveys and focus groups, failed to capture the full picture. The patient's voices remained a mystery, a treasure trove of insights locked away.

But a new technology was emerging, one with the potential to crack the code of online conversations. With its ability to analyze vast amounts of text data and identify emotional undercurrents, Sentiment analysis offered a way to listen to the patient uprising.

This book is the story of that transformation. It's about harnessing the power of sentiment analysis to unlock the hidden world of patient experience, using data to hear and understand patients, and building a future of healthcare where medications are developed with, not just for, patients.

The silent uprising has begun. Are you ready to listen?

THE PATIENT ODYSSEY
- A JOURNEY OF NEEDS AND FRUSTRATIONS

As the prologue recounts, Sarah's story is a microcosm of a larger phenomenon—the Patient Odyssey. This odyssey involves patients navigating the complexities of healthcare systems, battling insurance companies, and ultimately seeking medications that effectively address their needs.

This book delves deeper into the Patient Odyssey, exploring the challenges patients face at each stage:

- **Diagnosis and Information Overload:** The initial diagnosis can be a bewildering time. Patients are bombarded with medical jargon, treatment options, and often conflicting information online.
- **The Maze of Treatment Options:** Faced with a plethora of medications, patients struggle to understand their efficacy, side effects, and potential interactions with other medications.
- **The Hurdles of Affordability:** The financial burden of healthcare can be immense. Patients grapple with insurance coverage, co-pays, and the hidden costs of managing chronic illnesses.
- **The Silent Struggle with Side Effects:** Medications are not without their downsides. Patients often endure unpleasant side effects, impacting their daily lives and leading to feelings of isolation and frustration.
- **The Quest for Connection and Support:** Patients crave connection and support in these challenges. Online communities offer a safe space to share experiences, ask questions, and find solace in shared struggles.

Understanding the Patient Odyssey gives us a deeper appreciation of the emotional landscape patients navigate. This empathy is crucial for unlocking the true potential of sentiment analysis.

Beyond the Averages: Unveiling the Emotional Nuances

Traditional market research methods often rely on surveys and focus groups, providing a snapshot of average patient sentiment.

Sentiment analysis, however, allows us to delve deeper, uncovering the emotional tapestry woven within online conversations.

This book explores techniques for:

- **Identifying Emotional Tone:** Going beyond basic positive/negative sentiment, we can classify emotions like frustration, anxiety, hope, and relief.
- **Aspect-Based Sentiment Analysis:** This technique allows us to understand sentiment towards specific aspects of a medication, such as its effectiveness, side effects, or affordability.
- **Identifying Patient Personas:** By analyzing online conversations, we can segment patients into distinct personas based on their needs, concerns, and experiences.

These techniques paint a richer picture of the patient experience, allowing us to move beyond averages and truly understand the "why" behind patient sentiment.

Part I. Understanding Sentiment Analysis

Unveiling the Patient's Voice

Patient's voices echo through the digital ether, a symphony of experiences, anxieties, and hopes. But how do we capture the essence of these conversations? How do we translate the raw data of online reviews and social media posts into actionable insights that can revolutionize the pharmaceutical industry?

The answer lies in a powerful tool called sentiment analysis. This part of the book delves into sentiment analysis, equipping you with the knowledge and skills to unlock the treasure trove of patient insights hidden within online data.

We'll embark on a journey of discovery exploring the following:

- **The Fundamentals of Sentiment Analysis**: We'll break down the core concepts of sentiment analysis, understanding how it works to identify emotional tones within text data.
- **Traditional vs. Advanced Techniques**: We'll compare and contrast traditional lexicon-based analysis with more sophisticated machine learning approaches, highlighting each approach's strengths and limitations.
- **The Power of Natural Language Processing (NLP)**: In this section, we'll explore the role of NLP in sentiment analysis and examine how it enables computers to understand the nuances of human language.
- **Extracting the "Why" Behind Sentiment**: Going beyond basic positive or negative categorizations, we'll delve into techniques that reveal the emotions and motivations driving patient experiences.
- **The Challenges and Ethical Considerations**: No technology is without limitations. We'll discuss the challenges of sentiment analysis and explore ethical considerations when dealing with patient data.

By the end of Part I, you'll be equipped without a solid understanding of sentiment analysis and its potential to transform how pharmaceutical companies listen to and understand their patients.

CHAPTER 1

Introduction: The Voice of the Customer in Pharma

This chapter serves as the opening act, setting the stage for the book. Here is what you can expect to find:

1. **The Evolving Landscape of Pharma Marketing:**
   - This section will discuss how pharmaceutical companies market their products and how this is changing. It will likely touch upon the rise of the internet and social media, which have give n patients and healthcare providers (HCPs) a platform to share their experiences and opinions.
   - Traditional market research methods, such as surveys and focus groups, may need to be more effective at capturing online real-time conversations.
2. **Why Traditional Methods Fall Short:**
   - This section will explore the limitations of traditional market research methods. It might explain how surveys can be biased or have low response rates, and focus groups may not capture the full range of opinions.
3. **Introducing Sentiment Analysis: The New Voice of the Customer:**
   - Here, the chapter will introduce the concept of sentiment analysis and how it empowers pharma brand managers.
   - It will likely explain how sentiment analysis helps gather and analyze vast online conversations about pharmaceutical brands and competitors.

- This can provide valuable insights into people's thoughts and feelings, which can be difficult to capture with traditional methods.

Overall, Chapter One aims to convince the reader of the importance of sentiment analysis in today's digital pharma marketing landscape. It will likely paint a picture of how traditional methods struggle to keep up and how sentiment analysis offers a powerful new way to listen to the " voice of the customer."

1.1 The Evolving Landscape of Pharma Marketing and the Rise of Digital Influence

The evolving landscape of pharma marketing and the rise of digital influence is a key concept in understanding the importance of sentiment analysis in the pharmaceutical industry. Here are the details:

Evolving Landscape of Pharma Marketing

Traditional Pharma Marketing Strategies

- **Print Advertising**:
  - Pharmaceutical companies used to rely heavily on targeted advertisements in medical journals and publications. These publications were aimed at doctors and other healthcare professionals (HCPs). Ads often showcased new drugs, highlighted their benefits, and featured clinical trial data.
  - While this approach effectively reached doctors, it was a one-way communication channel. It didn't capture the real-time conversations happening online or gauge patient experience.
- **Sales Represenatatives**:
  - Pharmaceutical companies employed a network of sales representatives who visited doctor's offices directly. These representatives presented information about new medications, discussed their benefits, and answered questions.
  - This approach allowed for personalized doctor interaction but was expensive and limited in reach. Additionally, with the rise of evidence-based medicne, doctors became more reliant on independent research and less swayed by promotional visits.

- **Television Commercials**:
  - Pharmaceutical companies use television commercials to reach a broad audience, particularly during evening news programs. These commercials often presented a disease state and introduced the drug as a potential solution.

While this approach raised brand awareness, it could not effectively target specific patient groups and needed more clarity in conveying detailed information about medications and other potential side effects.

The Rise of Digital Influence

- **Empowered Patients**:
  - The internet has transformed how patients access information. They can now research their conditions, medications, and treatment options online. This empowers them to make more informed decisions about their healthcare.
  - Social media platforms like patient communities and support programs allow patients to connect, share experiences, and offer peer-to-peer support. These online conversations can influence treatment choices and brand perception.
- **Tech-Savvy Healthcare Professionals**:
  - Healthcare professionals (HCPs) increasingly use online resources for research and stay updated on new developments in their field. Medical journals now have online editions, and online databases provide access to the latest clinical trial data.
  - Social media allows HCPs to connect with colleagues globally, share knowledge, and participate in professional discussions. These online interactions can influence treatment protocols and brand reputation.

Impact on Pharma Marketing

- **Targeted Online Advertising**:
  - Pharma companies can use online advertising platforms to reach specific audiences based on demographics, online behavior (such as health-related searches), and medical conditions. This allows for much more targeted messaging compared to traditional methods.
  - Online advertising allows creative formats like video ads and interactive content to engage potential patients and HCPs.
- **Educational Content**:
  - Pharma companies can create valuable educational resources for patients and HCPs on disease treatment options. This content can be hosted on company websites, shared on social media platforms, and promoted through online advertising.
  - By providing evidence-based and informative content, pharma companies can build trust and establish themselves as leaders in their demographic areas.
- **Social Media Engagement**:
  - Pharma companies can utilize social media platforms to build communities and foster two-way communication with patients and HCPs. This can involve creating patient support groups, participating in relevant online discussions, and providing customer service through social media channels.
  - Pharma companies can gain valuable insights into patient needs, concerns, and perceptions of their products by actively engaging with the online community.

Understanding these shifts in the pharma marketing landscape highlights the limitations of traditional methods that don't consider the readily available "voice of the customer" through digital channels.

Sentiment analysis bridges this gap by analyzing online conversations and providing valuable insights into what patients and HCPs say about your brand and products.

1.2 Why Traditional Methods of Market Research Fall Short in the Digital Age

While still valuable in some contexts, traditional market research methods need help to keep pace with the fast-moving and dynamic nature of the digital age, especially in pharma marketing. Here is why:

Limitations of Traditional Methods:

A. Slow and Outdated:

- Traditional methods like surveys and focus groups often involve a multi-step process. Researchers must design the study, recruit participants, conduct interviews or surveys, and then analyze the data. This can take weeks or even months.
- When the results are available, the online landscape may have shifted significantly. New information, trends, and conversations may have emerged that traditional methods can't capture.
- The fast-paced nature of online communication demands a research approach that can keep up with the constant flow of information. Sentiment analysis tools can process vast amounts of data quickly and efficiently, providing near real-time insights.

B. Limited Scope:

- Traditional methods typically rely on a smaller sample size of participants, often recruited locally or through specific channels. This limits the generalizability of the findings and may not represent the full diversity of online opinions.
- The internet allows rich patient communities and geographically dispersed groups to connect and share experiences. Traditional methods struggle to reach these specific audiences and capture their unique perspectives.
- Sentiment analysis tools can analyze data from wider sources, including social media platforms, online forums,

and patient blogs. This allows for a more comprehensive understanding of the online conversation surrounding a brand or product.

C. **Superficial Data**:

- Surveys and focus groups often rely on self-reported data where participants consciously answer questions. This data can be biased or inaccurate for several reasons:
    - **Social Desirability Bias**: People may want to present themselves positively and be dishonest about their attitudes or behaviors.
    - **Recall Bias**: People may not accurately remember their past experiences or opinions.
    - **Limited Awareness**: People may only be conscious of some factors that influence their decisions.

Traditional methods may not capture the nuances of online conversations, where people express themselves more freely and openly. Sentiment analysis tools can analyze the language and context of the conversations to better understand the underlying attitudes and emotions.

The digital age presents unique challenges for market research:

- **Real-time Nature**:
    - Online conversations about pharmaceutical brands, products, and competitors occur 24/7. Traditional methods cannot keep up with this real-time flow of information.
    - Negative comments or concerns can spread quickly online, potentially damaging a brand's reputation. Sentiment analysis allows for continuous monitoring of online discussions, enabling pharmaceutical companies to identify and address issues quickly and effectively.
- **Volume and Variety**:
    - The internet generates vast amounts of data every day. This includes social media posts, online reviews, forum discussions, patient blogs, and more. Traditional methods

are not equipped to handle and analyze such large datasets effectively.

  - Manually coding and analyzing this data would be extremely time-consuming and labor-intensive. Sentiment analysis tools are designed to handle large volumes of text data and can identify trends and patterns that human analysis might miss.

- **Unsolicited Opinions**:
  - Unlike surveys and focus groups, where participants are prompted to give their opinions, online conversations are unsolicited and unfiltered. People are expressing their genuine thoughts and feelings without any external pressure.
  - Traditional methods might not capture these unfiltered opinions, leading to a less complete picture of how people perceive a brand or product. Sentiment analysis can analyze these unprompted expressions to understand the true feelings and perceptions of patients and HCPs. This allows pharmaceutical companies to gain valuable insights into what people are saying about their brand, medications, and competitors online, information that might be hidden in traditional methods.

Impact on Pharma Marketing

These limitations of traditional methods leave pharmaceutical companies with a significant blind spot when it comes to understanding the online conversations surrounding their brands and products. They may miss valuable insights about patient needs, concerns, and perceptions.

Sentiment analysis bridges this gap by providing real-time, in-depth insights into what patients and HCPs say online. This allows for more informed decision-making when it comes to:

- **Marketing Strategies**: Pharma companies can develop targeted marketing campaigns that resonate with their audience by understanding online sentiment. They can tailor messaging to address specific concerns and highlight the most important benefits to patients and HCPs.

- **Product Development**: Sentiment analysis can identify unmet medical needs and inform product development strategies. By understanding patient frustrations and challenges, pharmaceutical companies can develop new medications or improve existing ones to address patient needs better.

In conclusion, the digital age has fundamentally changed how people communicate and share information. Traditional market research methods struggle to keep pace with this evolving landscape. Sentiment analysis offers pharmaceutical companies a powerful tool for listening to the **voice of the customer** online and gaining valuable insights that can inform their marketing and product development strategies.

1.3 What is Sentiment Analysis and How it Empowers Pharma Brand Managers

Sentiment analysis is a powerful tool that helps pharma brand managers understand the **opinions, feelings, and attitudes** expressed online about their brand, products, and competitors. It analyzes vast amounts of data from various online sources and categorizes them as positive, negative, or neutral sentiment. Here is how it empowers pharma brand managers:

1. **Gain Customer Insights:**
    - **Traditional methods:** Like surveys and focus groups have limitations. Sentiment analysis provides real-time insights into what patients and healthcare professionals (HCPs) say about your brand and products online. This allows brand managers to understand their **unfiltered opinions and concerns**. Consider this for example: Imagine a pharma company relies on surveys to understand patient experiences with their new diabetes medication. Surveys may miss crucial aspects like side effects patients hesitate to report or unforeseen challenges with using the medicaiton.
    - **Uncover unmet needs**: By analyzing online conversations, brand managers can identify common patient frustrations and challenges related to existing medications or treatments. This valuable information can be used to develop new products that better address these unmet needs. For example, sentiment analysis of online forums and social media discussions might reveal patients frequently complaining about specific side effects of a popular mechanism of action that avoids those effects.

- **Identify patient journeys**: Sentiment analysis can help track how patients discuss a disease, their search for treatment options, and their medication experiences. This allows brand managers to understand the patient journey and tailor marketing messages accordingly. For instance, analyzing online reviews and patient blogs can reveal the typical path a patient with high blood pressure takes. They might start by searching for information about the condition, discuss treatment options with their doctor, and finally share their experiences with specific medications online. Understanding the patient journey allows brand managers to tailor educational content and marketing messages to each stage.

2. **Building Brand Reputation**:
   - **Monitor online conversations**: Sentiment analysis allows brand managers to monitor online discussions about their brand continuously. This enables them to address negative feedback proactively and prevent potential crises from developing. For instance, a pharma company launching a new pain medication might use sentiment analysis tools to track social media mentions and online reviews. This allows them to identify and address negative feedback about potential side effects or concerns about drug interactions quickly.
   - **Improve brand perception**: By understanding how patients and HCPs perceive the brand online, brand managers can develop strategies to improve brand perception and build trust. For instance, by analyzing online sentiment towards their brand compared to competitors, a pharma company developing a new cholesterol medicaiton can identify areas for improvement. They may discover that competitors are

perceived as more affordable or having fewer side effects. This insight can inform marketing strategies highlighting their medication's unique benefits and addressing perceived weaknesses.

3. **Optimizing Marketing Strategies**:
   - **Targeted campaigns**: Sentiment analysis reveals what resonates with patients and HCPs online. This allows brand managers to develop **targeted marketing campaigns** that use the right messaging and channels to reach the most relevant audiences. For instance, sentiment analysis of online forums for migraine sufferers might reveal a strong preference for natural remedies alongside prescription medicaiton. A pharma company developing a new migraine drug can then launch a targeted campaign on natural health websites and social media groups frequented by migraine sufferers.
   - **Improve content marketing**: Sentiment analysis can help understand which topics and formats are most engaging for patients and HCPs online. This allows brand managers to develop **effective content marketing strategies** that provide information and address audience needs. For example, analyzing the language used in online discussions about a particular disease can help identify the terminology patients use most often. A pharmaceutical company developing a new treatment for arthritis can use this information to create educational content that uses patient-centric language and addresses patients' specific concerns about the condition.
   - **Measure campaign effectiveness**: By tracking sentiment before, during, and after a marketing campaign, brand managers can measure its effectiveness and make adjustments needed. For example, a pharma company

launches a social media campaign promoting their allergy medication. They can measure the impact on brand perception by tracking sentiment before, during, and after the campaign. An increase in positive mentions and a decrease in negative sentiment indicates a successful campaign.

In conclusion, sentiment analysis empowers pharma brand managers with many customer insights that traditional methods can't capture. By understanding the online conversation, they can make data-driven decisions that improve brand reputation, optimize marketing strategies, and develop products and services that better serve patient needs.

CHAPTER

2

Demystifying Sentiment: The Science Behind Opinions

Imagine cracking the code of human emotions hidden within online text. Imagine understanding not just what patients say about medications but the "why" behind their opinions. This is the magic of sentiment analysis.

In this chapter, we delve into the science behind sentiment analysis, lifting the veil on the fascinating world of computational linguistics. We will explore how technology analyzes vast amounts of text data to identify and categorize emotional tones.

But is sentiment analysis simply a fancy algorithm counting positive and negative words? Not quite. Here is what you can expect to discover:

- **The Building Blocks of Sentiment Analysis**: This section will discuss the fundamental elements of sentiment analysis, including lexicons, machine learning algorithms, and natural language processing (NLP) techniques.
- **Lexicon-Based Analysis**: **A Simple Start:** We will begin by exploring lexicon-based analysis, which relies on pre-defined lists of words with positive, negative, or neutral sentiment associations.
- **Machine Learning Takes the Wheel**: We will then delve into machine learning, the workhorse behind advanced sentiment analysis. We will discuss how algorithms are trained on

massive datasets of labeled text data to identify compelling emotional patterns.

- **The Power of Context: Going Beyond Keywords**: You will learn how sentiment analysis goes beyond simply counting keywords. We will explore how context, sarcasm detection, and negation handling are crucial for accurate sentiment classification.
- **A Peek Under the Hood – Common Machine Learning Algorithms**: This chapter introduces some of the most common machine learning algorithms used in sentiment analysis and provides a basic understanding of their inner workings.

By the end of this chapter, you will gain a deep appreciation for the science behind sentiment analysis, demystifying the process of transforming online conversations into actionable patient insights. Get ready to unlock the secrets hidden within the world of patient opinions!

2.1 Understanding Different Types of Sentiment: Positive, Negative, and Neutral

Understanding different types of sentiment is fundamental to sentiment analysis. Here is a breakdown of the three main categories and how they might be applied to the pharmaceutical industry:

1. **Positive Sentiment**: This expresses satisfaction, approval, or happiness with a product, service, or experience. In the context of pharma, positive sentiment might look like:
   - **Direct Praise**: "This medication has been a lifesaver for my chronic pain."
   - **Recommendation**: "I would highly recommend this allergy medicaiton to anyone who suffers from seasonal allergies."
   - **Highlighting Benefits**: "This new diabetes treatment has helped me control my blood sugar levels without any side effects."
2. **Negative Sentiment**: This expresses dissatisfaction, disapproval, or frustration. In pharma, negative sentiment might be:
   - **Complaints About Side Effects**: "This medication makes me drowsy and dizzy all day."
   - **Ineffectiveness**: "This new treatment has not worked for my condition."
   - **Negative Experience**: "I had a terrible experience dealing with the customer service department for this medication."
3. **Neutral Sentiment:** This provides factual information or expresses no particular opinion. In pharma, neutral sentiment might include:
   - **Sharing Experiences:** "I just started taking this new medication for my high blood pressure. I will post an update in a few weeks."
   - **Seeking Information:** "Has anyone tried this new medication for migraines? I am curious about the side effects."

- Sharing News Articles: "Interesting article about the latest research on this new treatment for Alzheimer's disease."

Importance for Pharma Brand Managers:

Understanding these different types of sentiment allows pharma brand managers to:

- **Identify patient needs and concerns**: Positive sentiment highlights what patients like about existing treatments, while negative sentiment reveals areas for improvement.
- **Measure campaign effectiveness**: Tracking sentiment before, during, and after a marketing campaign shows whether it resonates with the target audience.
- **Improve brand reputation**: Pharma companies can build trust and improve brand perception by addressing negative sentiment and promoting positive experiences.

Some sentiment analysis tools go beyond positive and negative sentiment to detect **emotions** like frustration, hope, or gratitude in online conversations. This provides even deeper insights for pharmaceutical brand managers.

2.2 Exploring the Various Techniques Used in Sentiment Analysis: Lexicon-Based, Machine Learning and Deep Learning Approaches

Sentiment analysis employs various techniques to categorize text data as positive, negative, or neutral. Here is a breakdown of three common approaches:

1. **Lexicon-Based Analysis**:
   - Imagine a giant dictionary filled with words categorized by sentiment. This is the core of lexicon-based analysis.
   - **Process**:
     - A lexicon is a pre-defined list of words with assigned sentiment values (positive, negative, or neutral).
     - The sentiment analysis tool scans the text for these words and assigns a sentiment score based on the presence and frequency of these sentiment-laden words.
     - For example, if the text contains "excellent" (positive) and "terrible" (negative), the overall sentiment might be leaning positive.
   - **Advantages**:
     - Simple and easy to implement.
     - Relatively fast for processing large amounts of data and easy to understand
   - **Disadvantages**:
     - Limited in accuracy, especially for nuanced language or sarcasm.
     - Relies heavily on the quality and comprehensiveness of the lexicon.
     - Informal language (slang, emojis, abbreviations) can be misinterpreted.

2. **Machine Learning**:
    - This approach is like training a super-smart student to identify sentiment.
    - **Process**:
        - A machine learning algorithm is trained on a massive dataset of text labeled with sentiment (positive, negative, neutral).
        - The algorithm learns the patterns and relationships between words and their sentiment.
        - Once trained, the algorithm can analyze new text and predict its sentiment more accurately than a simple lexicon.
    - **Advantages**:
        - More accurate than lexicon-based analysis, especially for complex language.
        - It can adapt and improve over time as it is exposed to more data.
        - More flexible in handling informal language and slang.
    - **Disadvantages**:
        - Requires a large amount of labeled training data, which can be expensive and time-consuming to create.
        - The algorithm's inner workings can be a mystery, making it difficult to understand how it arrives at its sentiment classification.
3. **Deep Learning**:
    - This is like having a genius student with an extra powerful brain for sentiment analysis.
    - **Process**:
        - Deep learning utilizes complex neural networks inspired by the structure and function of the human brain.
        - These neural networks can analyze vast amounts of text data, identifying patterns and relationships between words, sentence structure, and even sarcasm.

    - Deep learning allows for more nuanced sentiment analysis, considering context and emotional undertones.
- **Advantages**:
    - Most accurate form of sentiment analysis, especially for complex language and sarcasm detection.
    - Can learn from vast amounts of data and improve over time.
- **Disadvantages:**
    - Requires significant computing power and resources.
    - Deep learning models can be even more opaque than machine learning, making it difficult to interpret their reasoning.

In conclusion, lexicon-based analysis is simple but less accurate. Machine learning offers a good balance between accuracy and complexity. Deep learning provides the most nuanced sentiment analysis but requires significant resources. Pharma companies can choose the technique that best suits their needs and resources. In the real world, these techniques are often combined for optimal results.

2.3 Factors Influencing Sentiment Analysis Accurately

Several factors can influence the accuracy of sentiment analysis, and pharma brand managers need to be aware of these limitations. Here are some key influencers:

1. **Informal Language**:
   - The internet is a breeding ground for informal language, slang, emojis, and abbreviations.
   - Sentiment analysis tools must be trained on such informal language to ensure accurate sentiment identification.
   - For example, "OMG, this medicine is amazing!" might be misinterpreted as a negative sentiment if the tool is unfamiliar with "OMG" as an expression of excitement.
2. **Sarcasm and Humor**:
   - Human communication relies heavily on sarcasm and humor, which can be difficult for sentiment analysis tools to grasp.
   - A statement like "This medication is a miracle cure," said with sarcasm might be misconstrued as a positive sentiment.
   - Advanced sentiment analysis tools use techniques such as considering context and sentence structure to improve sarcasm detection, but this remains a challenge.
3. **Context**:
   - Understanding the context of a conversation is crucial for accurate sentiment analysis.
   - A word like "great" could convey a positive sentiment about a medication's effectiveness but a negative sentiment about its side effects.
   - Sentiment analysis tools consider the surrounding words and sentences to understand the context better and assign the correct sentiment.

4. **Ambiguity**:
    - Language can be ambiguous, with words having multiple meanings depending on the context.
    - For example, "This medication is strong" could be positive (effective) or negative (harsh side effects).
    - Sentiment analysis tools are constantly improving to handle ambiguity but remain challenging.
5. **Quality of Training Data**:
    - Machine learning and deep learning approaches rely on large amounts of training data labeled with accurate sentiment.
    - The sentiment analysis tool will inherit these errors if the training data is biased or inaccurate.
    - Pharma companies should ensure their sentiment analysis tools are trained on high-quality data specific to the pharmaceutical industry and the languages used by their target audience.

By understanding these factors influencing accuracy, pharma brand managers can:

- **Set realistic expectations**: Sentiment analysis is a powerful tool, but it could be better.
- **Choose the right tool**: Consider the trade-off between accuracy and complexity when selecting a sentiment analysis tool.
- **Interpret results with caution:** Don't rely solely on sentiment analysis results. Combine them with other market research methods for a more complete picture.

Awareness of these limitations allows pharma to effectively use sentiment analysis to gain valuable insights from online conversations and improve brand strategies.

Part II. Why Sentiment Analysis Matters in Pharma

3. Building Brand Reputation in the Digital Age
4. Developing Patient-Centric Products
5. Optimizing Marketing and Communication Strategies
6. Staying Ahead of Competitive Intelligence Through Sentiment Analysis

Why does sentiment analysis matter for pharma companies in the digital age? Here are the details:

The Challenge: Traditional Market Research Falls Short

In today's digital world, traditional market research methods like surveys and focus groups have limitations that can hinder a pharma company's understanding of its target audience:

- **Slow and Outdated**: Traditional methods like surveys and focus groups rely on scheduled interactions, which cannot keep pace with the constant flow of online conversations. Thus, valuable insights about trending topics, sudden concerns, or emerging competitor discussions might be missed.
  - **Example**: A pharma company surveys patient experiences with their new diabetes medication. However, a few weeks later, online forums erupted with discussions about a previously unknown side effect. When the survey results are analyzed, the company has lost valuable time to address the issue.
- **Limited Scope**: Traditional methods often target specific demographics, potentially excluding niche patient communities or those hesitant to participate in formal research.
  - **Example**: A company developing a new treatment for a rare genetic disease might need help to recruit enough participants for a focus group. Sentiment analysis scans online support groups and forums frequented by these patients, revealing valuable insights into their needs and experiences.
- **Superficial Data**: Traditional methods rely on self-reported data, which can be biased or inaccurate. Patients may be reluctant to share negative experiences or downplay certain side effects.
  - **Example:** A survey asks patients to rate their satisfaction with a medication. While some may honestly report side effects, others might hesitate due to the fear of being judged or not wanting to seem ungrateful. Sentiment analysis can

analyze real-world discussions where patients openly share their experiences, potentially revealing a more complete picture.

The Solution:

Sentiment analysis helps pharma companies understand the "voice of the customer" online by analyzing vast amounts of textual data:

- **Real-Time Insights**: Sentiment analysis tools continuously monitor social media platforms, online reviews, and patient forums, providing real-time insights into what patients and HCPs say about the company, its products, and its competitors.
    - **Example**: A pharma company launches a new pain medication. Sentiment analysis allows them to track online mentions in real-time, identifying early concerns about potential side effects or patient experiences with the medication's effectiveness.
- **Unveiling Unsolicited Opinions**: It captures unfiltered opinions from patients and healthcare professionals (HCPs) that traditional methods might miss.
    - **Example**: By analyzing discussions on social media, a company might discover a growing frustration among patients regarding the high cost of their medicaiton. This valuable insight can inform pricing strategies or patient assistance programs.
- **Deeper Understanding**: It analyzes the language and context of conversations to understand underlying attitudes and emotions better.
    - **Example**: Analyzing online reviews of a new allergy medicaiton, sentiment analysis might not only identify negative sentiment about drowsiness as a side effect but also detect feelings of frustration or helplessness expressed by patients who struggle to manage their allergies effectively.

The Impact: Benefits for Pharma Marketing and Development

Sentiment analysis empowers pharma brand managers with valuable insights to make data-driven decisions:

- **Marketing Strategies**: Understanding online sentiment allows for developing targeted marketing campaigns that resonate with specific patient segments.
  - **Example**: Analysis of online discussions about a new migraine medication might reveal a strong preference for natural remedies used alongside prescription medication. The company can then launch a targeted campaign on wellness websites and social media groups frequented by migraine sufferers, highlighting the complementary benefits of their medication with natural approaches.
- **Product Development**: Sentiment analysis can identify unmet medical needs and inform product development strategies.
  - **Example**: Analyzing online forums for patients with arthritis might reveal a common complaint about the lack of effective pain relief options without harsh side effects. This valuable insight can guide the development of a new medication with a different mechanism of action that addresses this unmet need.
- **Brand Reputation Management**: Sentiment analysis allows for proactive online identification and management of negative feedback.
  - **Example**: A pharma company can use sentiment analysis tools to track mentions of their brand on social media. If negative sentiment emerges regarding a medication's side effects, the company can promptly issue a response addressing the concerns, potentially offering resources or clarifications. This proactive approach helps mitigate potential damage to brand reputation.

Here are some specific examples of how sentiment analysis benefits pharmaceutical companies:

- **Identifying unmet needs**: By analyzing online forums, a company might discover a frequent complaint about a common side effect of a particular medication. This could lead them to develop a new medication with a different mechanism of action to avoid that side effect.
- **Optimizing marketing campaigns**: Analyzing patient discussions about a disease can reveal the language they use and the information they seek. This allows targeted campaigns to use the right keywords and address their concerns.
- **Measuring Campaign Effectiveness**: Tracking sentiment before, during, and after a marketing campaign can show its impact on brand perception. An increase in positive mentions and a decrease in negative sentiment indicate a successful campaign.

Overall, sentiment analysis equips pharmaceutical companies to:

- **Stay ahead of the competition**: By understanding the online conversation, they can adapt their strategies to meet evolving patient needs.
  - **Example**: A company developing a new cholesterol-lowering medication might use sentiment analysis to track online discussions about competitor products. They can identify features patients value most and use this insight to differentiate their medication by highlighting its unique strengths.
- **Build stronger brand reputation**: By promptly addressing patient concerns and promoting positive experiences, healthcare providers can build trust and loyalty with their target audiences.
  - **Example**: A pharma company monitors sentiment analysis reports showing a positive increase in patient satisfaction following the launch of a new patient assistance program.

This valuable information can be used in future marketing campaigns to showcase their commitment to patient affordability and well-being.

- **Develop products and services that better serve patients**: By understanding patient needs and preferences expressed online, they can create solutions that make a difference in their lives.
    - **Example**: Analyzing online reviews of a new diabetes medicaiton, sentiment analysis might reveal a consistent theme of patients requesting a more user-friendly dosing schedule. This insight can inform the development of future medications with simple administration methods, improving patient adherence and overall treatment experience.

In conclusion, sentiment analysis is a powerful tool that helps pharma companies navigate the digital age and thrive in a competitive marketplace.

CHAPTER

3

Building Brand Reputation in the Digital Age

The digital age has transformed how pharmaceutical companies interact with patients and healthcare professionals (HCPs). Gone are the days of one-way communication through traditional media channels. Online conversations reign supreme today, making brand reputation management more crucial than ever. This chapter delves into how sentiment analysis empowers pharma companies to build a strong and positive brand reputation in the digital landscape.

The Power of Online Conversations

The internet has become a hub for healthcare information and discussions. Patients and HCPs actively use online platforms like:

- **Social media**: Sharing experiences, seeking advice, and discussing treatment options.
- **Online reviews**: Leaving feedback on medication and healthcare providers.
- **Patient forums**: Connecting with others who share similar conditions and exchanging support.
- **Healthcare news websites**: Staying updated on the latest medical research and developments.

These online conversations offer information about patient sentiment and brand perception. By analyzing these conversations through sentiment analysis, pharma companies can gain valuable insights into the following:

- **Patient needs and concerns**: Identifying common challenges patients face with their conditions and their expectations for treatment.
- **Perceptions of existing medications**: Understanding how patients view them, including their brands and competitors.
- **Emerging trends and discussions**: Staying abreast of the latest conversations about diseases, treatments, and healthcare in general.

Leveraging Sentiment Analysis for Reputation Management

Sentiment analysis empowers pharma companies to build and maintain a strong brand perception in several ways:

Proactively identifying issues: Sentiment analysis can help identify negative feedback about a product or service early by tracking online mentions. This allows for a swift and appropriate response, mitigating potential damage to brand reputation.

- **Addressing patient concerns**: Sentiment analysis can reveal specific concerns about side effects, medication efficacy, or affordability. Companies can proactively address these concerns through educational resources, patient support programs, or communication with HCPs.
- **Demonstrating responsiveness**: Responding promptly and professionally to negative online feedback showcases a company's commitment to patient well-being. Sentiment analysis efficiently identifies such feedback and facilitates timely responses.
- **Enhancing brand storytelling**: Positive online sentiment analysis about a company's products or services can be a powerful marketing tool. Sentiment analysis can help identify positive experiences and use them to craft compelling brand stories that resonate with patients and HCPs.

Here's an example: A pharma company launches a new medication for migraines. Through sentiment analysis, they discover online discussions where patients are frustrated with the medication's limited effectiveness and potential side effects. By proactively addressing these concerns, the company can:

- Issue a statement clarifying the medication's intended use and potential side effects.
- Offer resources for patients to discuss treatment options with their doctors.
- Engage with patients online to answer questions and gather feedback.

The company demonstrates responsiveness and transparency by taking these steps, potentially mitigating negative sentiment and building patient trust.

Building Trust Through Transparency

Transparency is key to building a strong brand reputation in the digital age. Here are some ways pharma companies can leverage sentiment analysis to promote transparency:

- **Addressing concerns openly:** By acknowledging and addressing negative feedback online, companies show they value patient experiences and are committed to improvement.
- **Providing accurate information**: Sentiment analysis can help identify areas where patients lack clear information about a medication. Companies can address this by developing educational resources or improving communication materials.
- **Engaging with patients and HCPs**: Actively participating in online conversations allows companies to provide accurate information, address concerns, and build trust with their target audience.

In conclusion, chapter three highlights how sentiment analysis empowers pharma companies to build and maintain a positive brand reputation in the digital age. By understanding online conversations, proactively addressing concerns, and promoting transparency, pharma companies can foster trust and build lasting relationships with patients and HCPs.

3.1 The Power of Online Conversations and the Impact on Brand Perception

Online conversations greatly shape pharmaceutical companies' brand perception in the digital age. Here is a breakdown of why these conversations matter and how they impact a brand's perception:

The Rise of Online Healthcare Discussions:

- Traditional media, like print ads and TV commercials, no longer hold the same sway. Today, patients and healthcare professionals (HCPs) actively engage in online discussions about health and medications on various platforms:
  - **Social Media**: Sharing experiences with medications, seeking advice from peers and medical professionals, and discussing treatment options.
  - **Online Reviews**: Leaving feedback on medications and healthcare providers, influencing the choices of others.
  - **Patient Forums**: Connecting with others facing similar conditions, offering and receiving support, and sharing insights about medications.
  - **Healthcare News Websites**: Staying informed about medical research, treatment breakthroughs, and industry developments.

Why Online Conversations Mater:

These online conversations create a powerful and dynamic space for shaping brand perception. They offer a wealth of unfiltered information about:

- **Patient needs and concerns**: What are the common challenges patients face with their conditions? What are their expectations from treatment options?
- **Perceptions of medications**: How do patients view existing medications, including a pharma company's brands and competitors? What are the perceived strengths and weaknesses?

- **Emerging trends and discussions**: What are the latest conversations about specific diseases, treatment approaches, and the healthcare landscape in general?

By analyzing these online conversations through sentiment analysis tools, pharma companies can gain valuable insights and understand the following:

- **Brand awareness**: How often is the brand mentioned online? In what context?
- **Brand sentiment**: Is the overall perception of the brand positive, negative, or neutral?
- **Strengths and weaknesses**: What are patients saying they like or dislike about the brand?

The Impact on Brand Perception

Online conversations can significantly influence brand perception in several ways:

- **Word-of-mouth effect**: Positive reviews and recommendations from patients and HCPs can build trust and encourage others to try a company's medications. Conversely, negative experiences shared online can damage brand reputation and deter potential patients.
- **Credibility and trust**: Companies that actively engage in online conversations, address concerns transparently, and provide accurate information can build trust and establish themselves as credible sources within the healthcare community.
- **Crisis Management**: Negative online sentiment can quickly escalate into a PR crisis. By monitoring online conversations, companies can identify potential issues early on and take steps to mitigate the damage.

Examples:

- A new allergy medication is being launched. Positive online reviews praising its effectiveness and minimal side effects can significantly boost brand perception and sales.

- A patient shares a negative experience with medication on social media, highlighting harsh side effects. If the company fails to acknowledge or address the concerns, it can damage brand trust and lead to negative online sentiment.

In conclusion, online conversations are a powerful force in the digital age. By harnessing their insights and actively engaging in these discussions, pharma companies can build a strong and positive brand reputation, fostering trust and loyalty among patients and HCPs.

3.2 Utilizing Sentiment Analysis to Identify and Address Brand Reputation Issues Proactively

In the fast-paced world of online conversations, sentiment analysis equips pharma companies to identify and address brand reputation issues before they snowball proactively. Here is how:

Early Warning Systems for Potential Problems:

- Sentiment analysis is a real-time monitoring tool that constantly scans online platforms like social media, review sites, and patient forums.
- By analyzing the sentiment of these conversations, the system can identify emerging negative feedback or concerns about a company's products, services, or even marketing campaigns.

Identifying Specific Issues:

- Sentiment analysis goes beyond just identifying positive or negative aspects. It can delve deeper to pinpoint the specific aspects causing concern.
- For example, negative sentiment about a medication might reveal patient frustrations with side effects, dosing instructions, or lack of affordability.

Taking Action Before It's Too Late:

- With early identification of potential problems, pharma companies can take proactive steps to address them before they escalate into major reputation issues. Here are some ways they can leverage this information:
- **Develop targeted responses**: Craft clear and informative responses to address specific concerns raised online. This demonstrates transparency and a commitment to patient well-being.
- **Improve communication strategies**: Identify areas where communication gaps exist and implement measures to address them. This might involve developing clearer medication

instructions, creating educational resources about side effects, or improving patient support programs.

- **Adapt marketing campaigns**: Sentiment analysis can reveal negative perceptions about a marketing message. Companies can adjust their approach to better resonate with the target audience and avoid amplifying negative sentiment.

Examples:

- A pharmaceutical company launches a new medication and, through sentiment analysis, discovers a surge of negative comments on social media about unexpected side effects.
    - **Proactive response**: The company can issue a statement clarifying the potential side effects and offering resources for patients to discuss with their doctors. They can also update their product information to ensure clear communication about potential side effects.
- A patient forum discussion reveals confusion about the dosage instructions for a particular medication:
    - **Proactive Response**: The company can analyze the conversation to understand the specific points of confusion. Then, it can develop clearer dosage instructions and update product labels or online resources to address the identified issue.

Benefits of Proactive Response:

By proactively addressing brand reputation issues, pharma companies enjoy several benefits:

- **Mitigate damage**: Swift action can prevent negative sentiment from spreading and potentially causing significant damage to brand reputation.
- **Build trust and transparency**: Proactive responses demonstrate a commitment to patient well-being and build trust with the target audience.
- **Improve brand image**: Addressing concerns head-on strengthens a company's brand image by demonstrating its willingness to listen, adapt, and improve.

In conclusion, sentiment analysis empowers pharma companies to act as proactive guardians of their brand reputation. Identifying potential issues early and taking swift action can prevent minor concerns from evolving into major crises, fostering trust and building a positive brand image in the digital age.

3.3 Case Study: How a Pharma Company Used Sentiment Analysis to Manage a Product Launch Crisis

The Scenario:

MegaPharm is a pharmaceutical company that launched a highly anticipated new medication, "Rejuvenate," to treat chronic fatigue syndrome (CFS). Pre-launch marketing campaigns generated significant excitement, with patients eager for a potential solution to their debilitating condition.

The Crisis:

Shortly after launch, MegaPharm starts noticing a surge of negative sentiment online. Patients on social media forums and review sites report experiencing severe headaches and dizziness as side effects of Rejuvenate. The initial sentiment surrounding the launch quickly turns into frustration and anger, with some patients accusing MegaPharm of misleading marketing and downplaying potential side effects.

Enter Sentiment Analysis:

MegaPharm recognizes the potential for a PR crisis and turns to its sentiment analysis tools. By analyzing online conversations, they gain valuable insights into the situation:

- **Identifying the Scope**: The sentiment analysis tool reveals a widespread issue with negative sentiment concentrated on headaches and dizziness as side effects.
- **Understanding Patient Concerns**: Analysis of the specific comments and reviews shows patients feel blindsided by these side effects and frustrated by a lack of clear information.

Taking Action:

Armed with these insights, MegaPharm implements a multi-pronged approach using the data from sentiment analysis:

- **Transparency and Communication**: MegaPharm publicly acknowledges the reported side effects. They emphasize the importance of consulting with a doctor for proper medication management and offer resources to address patient concerns about side effects.
- **Updating Information**: Based on the analysis of patient concerns, MegaPharm revises the medication's online information and product labeling to provide a more comprehensive picture of potential side effects.
- **Patient Support**: The company establishes a dedicated patient support hotline and an online forum to address patient concerns and provide personalized assistance.

The Outcome:

MegaPharma's swift and transparent response, guided by sentiment analysis data, helps mitigate the crisis. The negative sentiment online starts to subside as patients appreciate the company's acknowledgment of the issues and their efforts to address them. MegaPharm monitors online conversations to ensure clear communication and address any further concerns.

Lessons Learned:

This case study highlights the importance of sentiment analysis in managing product launch crises for pharmaceutical companies:

- **Early Detection**: Sentiment analysis allows for early identification of potential issues, enabling companies to take action before a minor problem escalates into a major crisis.
- **Understanding Patient Settlement**: By analyzing the "why" behind negative sentiment, pharma companies can identify specific concerns and tailor their responses accordingly.
- **Building Trust and Transparency**: Proactive communication and addressing patient concerns head-on fosters trust and transparency, allowing companies to navigate challenging situations more effectively.

In conclusion, this case study demonstrates how sentiment analysis gives pharmaceutical companies a valuable tool to manage product launch crises effectively. By harnessing the power of online conversations and responding transparently, companies can build trust with patients and protect their brand reputation.

CHAPTER 4

Developing Patient-Centric Products

The pharmaceutical industry is undergoing a significant shift towards patient-centricity. This chapter explores how sentiment analysis empowers companies to develop products that address patient needs to improve their healthcare experience.

The Traditional Approach: Limitations and Shortcomings

Traditionally, pharmaceutical companies have relied on a top-down approach to product development:

- **Focus on disease biology**: Research and development (R&D) efforts focused primarily on the underlying biological mechanisms of diseases.
- **Limited patient involvement**: Patient perspectives were often an afterthought, and real-world experiences and treatment burdens were minimally considered.
- **The gap between development and reality**: This approach sometimes resulted in products that, while effective in treating the core disease, needed to address the practical challenges patients face daily.

The Rise of Patient-Centricity:

The rise of patient advocacy groups and the increasing influence of online conversations have ushered in a new era of patient-centricity:

- **Focus on patient needs**: The emphasis has shifted to understanding the holistic experience of patients, including the physical symptoms, emotional well-being, and practical challenges associated with managing their condition.
- **Patient as a partner**: Patients are increasingly viewed as partners in the development process, providing valuable insights into their needs and preferences.

The Role of Sentiment Analysis:

Sentiment analysis plays a crucial role in developing patient-centric products by providing pharmaceutical companies with a wealth of patient data:

- **Identifying unmet needs**: Companies can analyze conversations in online forums and patient support groups to identify common pain points, frustrations, and unmet patient needs.
  - **Example**: Analysis of online conversations might reveal a strong demand for medication with fewer side effects or easier administration methods for a specific condition.
- **Understanding treatment burdens**: Sentiment analysis can illuminate patients' day-to-day challenges in managing their conditions. These might include medication adherence issues, worries about side effects, or difficulty accessing necessary resources.
  - **Example**: Analyzing online reviews of a new medication for diabetes might reveal concerns about the complexity of the dosing regimen, potentially hindering patient adherence.
- **Prioritizing product features**: By understanding patient preferences and priorities, companies can make informed decisions about product features.
  - **Example**: Sentiment analysis might show a strong preference for once-daily medications over multiple daily doses for a particular condition. Companies can then prioritize developing medications with this feature in mind.

Benefits of Patient-Centric Development:

Developing products with a patient-centric approach offers several benefits:

- **Improved patient outcomes**: Products designed around patient needs are more likely to be effective and manageable, leading to better patient outcomes.
- **Increased medication adherence**: When patients feel their voices are heard, and their needs are addressed, they are more likely to adhere to their treatment plans.
- **Enhanced brand reputation**: Companies committed to patient-centricity build trust and loyalty with patients, strengthening their brand reputation.

Examples of Patient-Centricity in Action:

- After analyzing online conversations, a pharmaceutical company developed a new asthma inhaler that revealed users' frustration with bulky and cumbersome traditional inhalers. The new inhaler is designed to be compact, user-friendly, and discreet.
- A company developing a new medicaiton for a chronic condition incorporates a mobile app based on insights from sentiment analysis. The app offers patients medication reminders, educational resources, and a platform to connect with other patients for support.

This chapter highlights how sentiment analysis empowers pharmaceutical companies to develop patient-centric products. By leveraging the vast amount of data available in online conversations, companies can gain a deeper understanding of patient needs and challenges. This patient-centric approach leads to developing more effective, manageable, and well-received products that improve patient outcomes and brand reputation.

4.1 Leveraging Sentiment Analysis to Gather Patient Feedback on Medications and Treatments

Traditionally, gathering patient feedback on medications and treatments relied on surveys, focus groups, and clinical trials. While valuable, these methods have limitations. Sentiment analysis offers a powerful alternative, providing real-time insights from a vast pool of patients in the digital age.

Limitations of Traditional Methods

- **Slow and Outdated**: Surveys and focus groups can take time to organize and analyze, hindering access to real-time patient experiences.
- **Limited Scope**: These methods often target specific demographics, potentially excluding niche patient communities or those hesitant to participate in formal research.
- **Superficial Data**: Traditional methods rely on self-reported data, which can be biased or lack the depth and detail of unfiltered online conversations.

Sentiment Analysis: A Powerful Tool for Patient Feedback

Sentiment analysis bridges the gap by analyzing vast amounts of textual data from online sources like:

- **Social Media Platforms**: Patients share their experiences with medications, discuss side effects, and exchange information about treatment options.
- **Online Review Sites**: Patients leave detailed reviews of medications, providing valuable insights into their effectiveness and ease of use.
- **Patient Forums and Support Groups**: Allow patients to connect with others facing similar conditions, offer and receive support, and share honest experiences with medications.

- **Healthcare News Websites**: Comment sections on healthcare news articles reveal patient perspectives on new treatments and ongoing research.

Benefits of Sentiment Analysis for Patient Feedback

- **Real-Time Insights**: Sentiment analysis tools continuously monitor online conversations, providing access to real-time feedback on medications or treatments.
- **Unfiltered Opinions**: Online platforms allow for unfiltered patient experiences, revealing valuable insights beyond what traditional methods might capture.
- **Deeper Understanding**: Sentiment analysis goes beyond just positive or negative sentiment. It can analyze the language and context of conversations to understand patients' underlying emotions, concerns, and needs.

Examples of Leveraging Sentiment Analysis

- **Identifying Side Effects**: By analyzing online reviews of a new medicaiton, sentiment analysis might reveal previously unknown but commonly reported side effects. This allows companies to investigate further and potentially update medication information or warnings.
- **Understanding Treatment Burden**: Analyzing online forums for patients with a chronic condition might reveal concerns about the complexity of a treatment regimen. This can inform the development of patient support programs or educational resources to improve medication adherence.
- **Prioritizing Feature Development**: Sentiment analysis of online discussions about diabetes medications might show a strong preference for once-daily medications. Companies can then prioritize research and development of medications with this feature.

Overall, Sentiment analysis empowers pharmaceutical companies to:

- **Develop more effective treatments**: That address real-world concerns and improve patient outcomes.
- **Improve Medication Adherence**: When patients feel their experiences are acknowledged and their needs are considered, they are more likely to adhere to their treatment plans.
- **Build Trust and Transparency**: Gathering and responding to patient feedback through sentiment analysis demonstrates a commitment to patient well-being focus, and trust in with the target audience.

In conclusion, sentiment analysis offers a revolutionary approach to gathering patient feedback on medication treatments. By harnessing the power of online conversations, pharmaceutical companies can gain valuable insights, make data-driven decisions, and develop products and services that truly serve patients' needs.

4.2 Identifying Unmet Medical Needs and Opportunities for Product Development

The pharmaceutical industry thrives on innovation, constantly seeking to develop new medications and treatments that address unmet medical needs. In this ever-evolving field, sentiment analysis emerges as a powerful tool for identifying these needs and pinpointing potential opportunities for product development.

The Challenge: Traditional Methods Fall Short

Traditionally, pharmaceutical companies have relied on methods like:

- **Clinical Trials**: While valuable, these can be expensive, time-consuming, and limited in scope.
- **Market Research**: Surveys and focus groups might miss crucial insights from niche patient committees or those hesitant to participate formally.
- **Physician Feedback**: Doctors provide valuable input, but their perspectives might not fully encompass patients' experiences.

Sentiment Analysis: A Window into Patient Needs

Sentiment analysis unlocks a treasure a wealth of patient experiences and perspectives through online conversations:

Social media platforms: Patients share experiences with existing medications, discuss challenges with their conditions, and express desires for new treatment options.

- **Patient forums and support groups**: Patients connect with others facing similar conditions, offering and receiving support and openly discussing unmet needs and treatment limitations.
- **Online review sites**: Reviews of medications and healthcare providers offer insights into patient satisfaction and areas of improvement.
- **Healthcare news websites**: Comment sections on articles reveal patient reactions to new research and ongoing discussions about disease management.

How Sentiment Analysis Reveals Unmet Needs

By analyzing the vast amount of textual data in these online platforms, sentiment analysis helps identify unmet needs in several ways:

- **Recurring Complaints**: Sentiment analysis can identify recurring themes of frustration or dissatisfaction with existing treatments. These might point to limitations in effectiveness, side effects, or difficulty with administration.
    - **Example**: Analysis of online forums for patients with chronic pain might reveal widespread complaints about the limited efficacy of current medications and the presence of undesirable side effects. This indicates a potential need for new pain management options with fewer side effects and better pain control.
- **Expression of Desire**: Patients often desire specific features in a medication or treatment. These desires can be related to treatment duration, ease of use, or specific delivery methods.
    - **Example**: Analyzing social media discussions about diabetes management might reveal a strong demand for long-acting insulin that requires fewer daily injections. This indicates an opportunity to develop a new insulin formulation that addresses this need.
- **Gaps in Treatment Options**: Sentiment analysis can reveal situations where existing treatments only address certain aspects of a condition, leaving other patient needs unmet.
    - **Example**: Analyzing online forums for patients with a particular mental health condition might show concerns about the lack of medications that address both emotional and cognitive symptoms. This suggests a potential need for a new class of medications with a broader spectrum of action.

Benefits of Identifying Unmet Needs

- **Targeted Innovation**: By understanding unmet needs, companies can focus research and development efforts on areas with the greatest potential to improve patient outcomes.
- **Developing Effective Treatments**: New medications and treatments can be designed to address patients' specific needs and challenges, leading to more effective solutions.
- **Enhanced Patient Satisfaction**: Products that address unmet needs are more likely to be well-received by patients, improving overall treatment satisfaction and adherence.

Examples of Unmet Needs Leading to Innovation

- Sentiment analysis might reveal a strong demand for migraine medications with fewer side effects and faster-acting relief. This could lead to the development of new drug delivery systems or medications with novel mechanisms of action.
- Analysis of online discussions about managing chronic illnesses might indicate a need for more patient-friendly medication administration methods. This could inspire the development of easy-to-use self-injection devices or digital medication reminders.

In conclusion, sentiment analysis equips pharmaceutical companies to identify unmet medical needs with unprecedented clarity. By harnessing the power of online conversations, companies can gain valuable insights into patient experiences and aspirations. This, in turn, fuels innovation and leads to the development of new and improved medications and treatments that truly serve patients' needs.

4.3 Case Study: A Pharma Company Using Sentiment Analysis to Inform Patient-Centric Drug Design

The Scenario:

Zenith Pharmaceuticals, a leading drug development company, aims to create a new medication for irritable bowel syndrome (IBS), a chronic condition affecting millions worldwide. IBS symptoms can vary greatly from person to person, making it challenging to develop a one-size-fits-all solution.

The Challenge:

Zenith traditionally relied on clinical trials and physician feedback to understand patient needs and inform their drug design process. They analyze online conversations across various platforms like:

- **Patient forums**: Patients openly discuss challenges with current medications, desired treatment features, and specific IBS symptoms that significantly impact their daily lives.
- **Social media**: Patients share experiences and frustrations with existing treatments and desire new management options.
- **Online review sites**: Reviews of IBS medications offer insights into patient satisfaction with existing treatments and areas for improvement.

Insights from Sentiment Analysis

By analyzing online conversations, Zenith uncovers valuable information:

- **Unmet Needs**: Patients express frustration with the limited effectiveness of current IBS medications, highlighting the need for a treatment that offers broader symptom relief.
- **Symptom Variations**: Sentiment analysis reveals a diverse range of IBS symptoms impacting patients, including bloating, cramping, and irregular bowel movements.

- **Treatment Burden**: Patients discuss challenges with side effects, complex medicaiton schedules, and the desire for a more convenient treatment option.

Informing Drug Design

Armed with these insights, Zenith adopts a patient-centric approach to drug design:

- **Multi-Symptom Targeting**: The new medication formulation addresses a broader range of IBS symptoms, aiming for more comprehensive symptom relief.
- **Tailored Dosing**: Considering the concerns about complex medication schedules, Zenith explores options for flexible dosing regimens based on individual patient needs.
- **Reduced Side Effects**: Understanding patient concerns about side effects, Zenith prioritizes the development of a medication with a lower side-effect profile.

Patient Engagement

Zenith goes beyond analysis and actively engages with patient communities online:

- **Focus Groups**: Zenith conducts online focus groups with IBS patients to gather further feedback on their proposed drug design approach.
- **Online Surveys**: They use online surveys to gauge patient preferences for medication delivery methods and dosing schedules.

The Outcome:

Through sentiment analysis and patient engagement, Zenith develops a new IBS medication with the following features:

- **Improved symptom control**: The medication targets a wider range of IBS symptoms, improving patients' overall relief.

- **Flexible Dosing**: Patients have more control over their medicaiton schedule with a tailored dosing regimen based on individual needs.
- **Reduced Side Effects**: The new formulation prioritizes minimizing potential side effects, enhancing patient tolerability.

Lessons Learned

This case study highlights the power of sentiment analysis in informing patient-centric drug design:

- **Understanding Patient Needs**: Sentiment analysis provides a comprehensive understanding of patient experiences and unmet needs, concerns, and preferences, leading to more effective treatments.
- **Focusing on Patient Outcomes**: By prioritizing patient needs, concerns, and preferences, drug development is directed toward improving patient well-being and treatment satisfaction.
- **Engaging with Patients**: Active patient engagement throughout development ensures that the final product meets patient expectations and addresses their specific challenges.

In conclusion, this case study demonstrates how sentiment analysis empowers pharmaceutical companies to develop patient-centric medications. By harnessing the power of online conversations and patient engagement, companies can design drugs that address real-world needs and improve the lives of millions who struggle with chronic conditions.

CHAPTER

5

Optimizing Marketing and Communication Strategies

The digital age has revolutionized how pharmaceutical companies reach and engage with patients and healthcare professionals (HCPs). Traditional marketing channels are needed. This chapter explores how sentiment analysis empowers pharma companies to develop data-driven marketing and communicate strategies that resonate with their target audience.

The Evolving Landscape of Pharma Marketing

- **Shifting Patient Behavior**: Patients increasingly use online resources for health information and treatment options.
- **Rise of Social Media**: Social media platforms have become hubs for patient discussions and HCP engagement.
- **Demand for Transparency and Authenticity**: Patients and HCPs expect clear, transparent communication from pharmaceutical companies.

The Challenges of Traditional Marketing

Traditional marketing methods, such as television commercials and print ads, are often:

- **One-way communication**: Limited opportunities for interactive engagement with patients and HCPs.
- **Broad targeting**: Difficulty in reaching specific patient demographics or tailoring messages to individual needs.

- **Limited data insights**: Traditional methods offer minimal data on audience reception and campaign effectiveness.

Sentiment Analysis: A Game Changer for Pharma Marketing

Sentiment analysis equips pharma companies to develop effective marketing and communication strategies in several ways:

- **Understanding Audience Needs**: By analyzing online conversations, companies gain insights into patient concerns, treatment preferences, and information gaps. This allows them to develop targeted and relevant marketing messages.
  - **Example**: Sentiment analysis reveals high online searches for information about a specific disease. A pharmaceutical company can develop a targeted marketing campaign offering educational resources and addressing common patient questions.
- **Identifying Influential Voices**: Sentiment analysis can help identify HCPs and patient advocates with a strong online presence and credibility. These influencers can be valuable partners in promoting disease awareness and treatment options.
  - **Example**: Analysis of social media discussions about a new medication might reveal a cardiologist who consistently shares informative content and engages with patients. The pharma company can partner with this cardiologist to develop educational content about the medication.
- **Optimizing Campaign Performance**: Sentiment analysis allows for real-time monitoring of online conversations about marketing campaigns. This provides valuable insights into audience reception and helps companies identify areas for improvement or adjust messaging on the fly.
  - **Example**: A pharma company launches a social media campaign about a new medication. Sentiment analysis reveals negative feedback about the campaign's tone or lack of clarity. The company can adjust the campaign messaging to better resonate with the target audience.

- **Building Brand Trust**: Pharma companies can build trust and credibility with their audience by engaging in online conversations, addressing concerns transparently, and providing accurate information.

Benefits of Data-Driven Marketing

- **Increased Campaign Effectiveness**: Marketing messages are tailored to specific audience needs and preferences, leading to higher engagement and campaign success.
- **Improved Patient Education**: Targeted educational content empowers patients to make informed decisions about their health and treatment options.
- **Stronger Relationships with HCPs**: Collaboration with HCP influencers fosters trust and promotes the effective use of medications within the healthcare community.

Examples of Data-Driven Marketing Strategies

- A pharma company develops a series of educational videos addressing common patient concerns about a specific condition based on insights from sentiment analysis.
- A company partners with a patient advocacy group to launch a social media campaign to promote disease awareness and encourage patients to seek early diagnosis.
- Sentiment analysis of online discussions about a new medication reveals a need for more detailed information on its side effects. The company develops a comprehensive FAQ section to address this need on its website.

In conclusion, this chapter highlights how sentiment analysis empowers pharmaceutical companies to develop data-driven marketing and communication strategies. By leveraging the power of online conversations, companies can gain valuable audience insights, create targeted campaigns, and build stronger relationships with patients and HCPs. This ultimately leads to improved patient education, brand trust, and successful marketing initiatives in the ever-evolving digital landscape.

5.1 Understanding How Patients and HCPs Feel About Your Brand Messaging

Pharmaceutical companies must understand how patients and healthcare professionals (HCPs) perceive their brand messaging in the digital age. Traditionally, gauging audience sentiment relied on surveys, focus groups, and limited feedback channels. Sentiment analysis offers a powerful alternative, providing real-time insights into how your brand messaging resonates with your target audience.

Why Understanding Perception Matters

- **Impact on Brand Image**: How patients and HCPs perceive your messaging shapes their overall impression of your brand. Positive sentiment builds trust and credibility, while negative sentiment can damage a brand's reputation.
- **Campaign Effectiveness**: If your messaging misses the mark, it won't resonate with your audience, and your campaign won't achieve its goals.
- **Identifying Areas for Improvement**: Understanding audience sentiment allows you to refine your messaging strategy, address shortcomings, and ensure it aligns with your target audience's needs and expectations.

Sentiment Analysis: A Window into Audience Perception

Sentiment analysis unlocks a vast amount of data from online conversations:

- **Social media platforms**: Patients and HCPs share their thoughts and feelings about brand messaging on platforms like Twitter (X now), Facebook, and professional networking sites.
- **Online reviews and forums**: Reviews of your medications and discussions on healthcare forums can reveal insights into how patients perceive your brand communication.

- **News websites and articles**: Comment sections on healthcare news articles can provide valuable feedback on how HCPs view your brand messaging within the context of new research or treatment options.

How Sentiment Analysis Reveals Perception

By analyzing the language used and the context of online conversations, sentiment analysis goes beyond simply positive or negative. It helps you understand:

- **Emotional Tone**: Does your messaging evoke trust, hope, or frustration?
- **Clarity and Understanding**: Do patients and HCPs need clarification on your message, or do they find it clear and informative?
- **Messaging Relevance**: Does your messaging address the needs and concerns of your target audience?
- **Brand Image Perception**: How is your brand portrayed in online conversations? Is it seen as reliable, innovative, or misleading?

Examples of Using Sentiment Analysis

- A pharma company launches a social media campaign promoting a new medication. Sentiment analysis reveals positive feedback about the message's optimistic tone but identifies concerns about the lack of information on side effects. The company can adjust the campaign to address these concerns.
- Online medication review analysis reveals patient confusion regarding the medication's dosage instructions. This can indicate a need for clearer communication on product labeling and marketing materials.
- Sentiment analysis of comments on a news article about a new drug discovery shows HCPs expressing skepticism about

the company's claims. This might prompt the company to focus on providing more data and scientific evidence to support its messaging.

Benefits of Understanding Audience Perception

- **Improved Brand Messaging**: By understanding how your messaging is received, you can refine it to resonate better with your target audience, leading to more effective communication.
- **Building Trust and Credibility**: Responding to concerns and addressing audience feedback demonstrates transparency and builds trust with patients and HCPs.
- **Optimizing Marketing Campaigns**: Sentiment analysis allows for real-time adjustments to ongoing campaigns, ensuring they deliver the intended message and achieve desired outcomes.

In conclusion, sentiment analysis empowers pharmaceutical companies to gain valuable insights into how patients and HCPs perceive their brand messaging. This allows for data-driven communication strategies that build trust, improve brand image, and lead to successful marketing initiatives in the digital age.

5.2 Tailoring Marketing Campaigns Based on Sentiment Analysis to Resonate with Target Audiences

In the age of digital communication, pharmaceutical companies need to ensure their marketing campaigns resonate with patients and healthcare professionals (HCPs). Here is how sentiment analysis can be used to tailor campaigns for maximum impact:

Understanding Your Audience

The first step is to gain a deep understanding of your target audience. Sentiment analysis helps you achieve this by:

- **Identifying Concerns and Needs**: Analyze online conversations on social media, forums, and review sites. This reveals patients' concerns, needs, and information gaps regarding your treatment area.
  - **Example**: Sentiment analysis of conversations about a new diabetes medication might reveal a strong patient desire for once-daily dosing.
- **Gauging HCP Perception**: Analyze comments on news articles and professional networking sites to understand how HCPs view your brand and its place within the treatment landscape.

Tailoring Your Message

With a clear understanding of your audience, you can craft targeted messages:

- **Addressing Patient Needs**: Highlight aspects of your medication or treatment that directly address the concerns and needs identified through sentiment analysis.
  - **Example**: If patients struggle with multiple daily injections for diabetes, your campaign could emphasize the convenience of your once-daily medicaiton.

- **Language and Tone**: Sentiment analysis can help you identify your audience's preferred communication style. Use clear, informative language that resonates with their emotions (e.g., hopeful, frustrated).
- **Segmentation**: Sentiment analysis might reveal different needs within your target audience. Tailor your message accordingly, creating segmented campaigns for specific patient demographics or HCP specialties.

Platforms and Channels

Sentiment analysis helps you choose the most effective platforms to reach your audience:

- **Social Media**: Target specific patient communities or HCP groups based on their online activity and discussions.
- **Educational Resources**: Develop targeted educational content (videos, articles) addressing the specific questions and information gaps revealed through sentiment analysis.
- **Targeted Advertising**: Leverage online advertising platforms to reach patients and HCPs interested in your treatment area based on their online behavior.

Monitoring and Refinement

Sentiment analysis is an ongoing process that allows for real-time campaign adjustments:

- **Tracking Audience Response**: Monitor online conversations throughout the campaign to see how your message is received.
- **Addressing Concerns**: If sentiment analysis reveals negative feedback, address those concerns promptly and transparently.
- **Optimizing Messaging**: Refine your message on the fly based on audience reaction, ensuring it continues to resonate with your target audience.

Benefits of Tailored Messaging

- **Increased Campaign Effectiveness**: Targeted messaging based on audience needs leads to higher engagement and campaign success.
- **Building Trust and Credibility**: Your brand builds trust and credibility by addressing patient concerns and demonstrating an understanding of HCP needs.
- **Improved Patient Outcomes**: Effective communication empowers patients to make informed decisions about their health and treatment options.

Examples of Tailored Marketing Campaigns

- A pharmaceutical company used sentiment analysis to learn that patients with chronic conditions struggle with managing complex medication schedules. To address this, the company launched a social media campaign focusing on its medication's ease of use, featuring testimonials from patients who found it simplified their daily routines.
- Sentiment analysis reveals that HCPs are hesitant about a new medication due to a lack of long-term efficacy data. The company tailors its marketing materials to HCPs, providing detailed clinical trial results and scientific evidence to address their concerns.

In conclusion, sentiment analysis empowers pharmaceutical companies to tailor marketing campaigns that resonate with the specific patient and HCP audiences. By understanding their needs, concerns, and preferred communication styles, companies can craft targeted messages that are informative and engaging, leading to successful marketing initiatives and improved patient outcomes.

5.3 Case Study: A Pharma Company Leveraging Sentiment Analysis to Improve the Effectiveness of their Patient Education Materials

The Scenario

Clarion Pharmaceuticals, a leading provider of medications for chronic respiratory conditions, aims to improve the effectiveness of its patient education materials. While it offers brochures, online resources, and support groups, patient feedback suggests these materials do not meet all patients' needs.

The Challenge

Traditionally, Clarion relied on surveys and focus groups to gather feedback on their patient education materials. However, these methods have limitations:

- **Limited Scope**: Surveys and focus groups only reach a small sample of patients, potentially missing crucial insights from broader demographics.
- **Social Desirability Bias**: Patients might hesitate to express negative feedback in a formal setting.
- **Lack of Real-Time Insights**: Traditional methods are slow and don't provide real-time feedback on how patients interact with the educational materials.

The Solution: Sentiment Analysis

Clarion leveraged sentiment analysis to better understand how patients interact with their educational materials. They analyzed online conversations across various platforms:

- **Social media posts**: Patients discuss challenges they face managing their condition, their experiences with medications, and the resources they find helpful.

- **Online reviews**: Reviews of Clarion's medications might offer insights into patients' struggles with understanding medication instructions or using specific devices.
- **Patient forums**: Forums offer a platform for patients to share experiences, ask questions, and express frustrations about their condition and treatment options.

Insights from Sentiment Analysis

By analyzing online conversations, Clarion uncovers valuable information:

- **Content Gaps**: Sentiment analysis reveals areas where patients lack clarity or find the information insufficient. For example, patients might express confusion about specific medication side effects or difficulty using inhalation devices.
- **Delivery Preferences**: Analysis shows some patients prefer video tutorials over written instructions, while others might benefit from interactive quizzes to test their understanding.
- **Emotional Tone**: Online conversations reveal patient anxieties, frustrations, and the desire for more empathetic and supportive educational materials.

Tailoring Educational Materials

Armed with these insights, Clarion personalizes its patient education approach:

- **Content Revamp**: They revive existing brochures and online resources to address identified content gaps. Information is presented more clearly, and complex topics are broken down into simpler language.
- **Multimedia Resources**: Clarion developed video tutorials demonstrating proper medication usage and inhalation techniques, catering to patients who prefer visual learning.
- **Interactive Elements**: They incorporated quizzes and interactive tools into their online resources to enhance patient engagement and knowledge retention.

- **Empathetic Tone**: The educational materials are rewritten with a more empathetic and supportive tone, acknowledging patient challenges and offering encouragement.

Measuring Success

Clarion continues to monitor online conversations to gauge the impact of its revamped educational materials:

- **Increased Positive Sentiment**: They track an increase in positive online comments about the clarity and helpfulness of their educational resources.
- **Reduced Patient Confusion**: Sentiment analysis reveals a decrease in online discussions about confusion regarding medication use or side effects.
- **Improved Patient Engagement**: Metrics show increased user engagement with the new interactive elements within Clarion's online resources.

Lessons Learned

This case study highlights the value of sentiment analysis in improving patient education materials:

- **Understanding Patient Needs**: Sentiment analysis provides real-time insights into patient needs and challenges, ensuring educational materials address their specific concerns.
- **Personalized Learning**: Clarion offers various formats and interactive elements to accommodate different learning styles and preferences.
- **Building Trust and Support**: Empathetic and informative educational materials foster trust and empower patients to manage their condition effectively.

In conclusion, this case study demonstrates how sentiment analysis empowers pharmaceutical companies to create truly helpful and engaging patient education materials. By understanding patient needs and preferences, companies can develop resources that improve understanding, reduce confusion, and improve health outcomes.

CHAPTER 6

Staying Ahead of Competitive Intelligence Through Sentiment Analysis

Staying ahead of the competition is crucial for success in the pharmaceutical industry. This chapter explores how sentiment analysis equips companies with valuable insights into competitor activity, patient perceptions, and emerging trends, allowing them to develop effective competitive intelligence strategies.

The Competitive Landscape

The pharmaceutical industry is highly competitive, with companies constantly striving to:

- Develop innovative new medications and treatments.
- Capture market share.
- Position themselves favorably in the eyes of patients and healthcare professionals (HCPs).

Traditional Competitive Intelligence Methods

Traditionally, companies relied on methods like:

- **Market research reports:** These reports offer valuable information but can be expensive and need more real-time insights.
- **Monitoring competitor marketing materials:** Provides limited information on patient and HCP perceptions.

- **Attending industry conferences:** Offers a snapshot of competitor strategies but might need to catch broader trends in patient needs.

The Power of Sentiment Analysis:

Sentiment analysis provides a powerful tool for gathering competitive intelligence in the digital age:

- **Real-Time Insights**: Sentiment analysis monitors real-time online conversations, offering up-to-date information on competitor activity and patient perceptions.
- **Unfiltered Opinions**: Online platforms allow patients and HCPs to share unfiltered opinions on competitor medications, treatments, and marketing strategies.
- **Broader Scope**: Sentiment analysis goes beyond a single competitor, allowing you to monitor the entire industry landscape and identify emerging trends.

Applications of Sentiment Analysis for Competitive Intelligence

- **Understanding Patient Perception of Competitor Products**: Analyze online reviews, forums, and social media discussions to understand patient experiences with competitor medications. This can reveal areas of weakness (e.g., side effects, complex dosing) to exploit and inform your product development efforts.
    - **Example**: Sentiment analysis might reveal widespread patient complaints about a competitor's medication's high rate of unpleasant side effects. This information can inform the development of your medication, which should focus on minimizing side effects.
- **Tracking Competitor Marketing Campaigns**: Monitor online conversations surrounding competitor marketing campaigns. This allows you to assess their effectiveness, identify weaknesses, and develop targeted counter-messaging strategies.

  - **Example**: Analysis might show negative sentiment towards a competitor's marketing campaign for a new medication due to misleading claims. You can develop a campaign highlighting your medications' transparency and data-driven approach.
- **Identifying Emerging Trends in Treatment Options**: You can identify emerging patient needs and treatment preferences by analyzing online discussions about specific diseases or conditions. This allows you to adapt your research and development efforts to address these evolving needs and potentially get ahead of the competition.
  - **Example**: Sentiment analysis might reveal a growing interest in alternative treatment options for a particular condition. To meet this demand, you can explore the development of complementary therapies or natural remedies.

Competitive Intelligence Benefits

- **Informed Decision-Making**: Sentiment analysis provides valuable data to support strategic decisions regarding product development, marketing campaigns, and overall competitive positioning.
- **Identifying Opportunities**: By understanding patient needs and emerging trends, companies can identify new market opportunities and develop innovative solutions to address unmet medical needs.
- **Building a Strong Brand Reputation**: By leveraging insights from sentiment analysis, companies can refine their messaging and address patient concerns, ultimately building a strong brand reputation within the competitive landscape.

Examples of Competitive Intelligence Strategies

- A pharma company uses sentiment analysis to learn that a competitor's medication for a specific condition has a complex dosing regimen, leading to patient frustration. They develop a new medicaiton with a simpler and more convenient dosing schedule, highlighting the advantage in their marketing campaigns.

- Sentiment analysis reveals a growing trend of HCPs discussing the potential of a new drug class for a particular disease. The company prioritizes research and development efforts in this area, aiming to be the first to market a medication within this new class.

Conclusion

This chapter emphasizes how sentiment analysis empowers pharmaceutical companies to gather valuable competitive intelligence in the digital age. By harnessing the power of online conversations, companies can gain insights into competitor activity, patient perceptions, and emerging trends. This knowledge empowers them to make informed decisions, identify new opportunities, and ultimately stay ahead of the competition to develop innovative, effective medications that serve patients' needs.

6.1 Benchmarking Your Brand Against Competitors in the Online Space

Understanding how your brand stacks up against the competition online is crucial in the competitive world of pharmaceuticals. Benchmarking allows you to assess your performance, identify areas for improvement, and ultimately develop a winning digital strategy.

Why Online Benchmarking Matters

- **The Digital Patient Journey**: Patients increasingly turn to online resources for information, reviews, and support regarding medications and treatment options. Your online presence significantly impacts your brand perception.
- **Competitive Landscape**: Understanding how your competitors leverage the online space allows you to identify best practices and potential weaknesses to exploit.
- **Data-Driven Decisions**: Benchmarking provides objective data to guide your online strategy, ensuring your brand messaging and communication resonate with your target audience.

Traditional Benchmarking Methods

Traditionally, companies relied on limited methods for online benchmarking;

- **Website traffic analysis**: Offers basic insights into website visits but needs more context on user engagement or competitor performance.
- **Manual competitor analysis**: Time-consuming and subjective process of analyzing competitor websites and social media presence.
- **Limited market research reports** can be expensive and may not provide an in-depth analysis of the online landscape.

The Power of Online Benchmarking Tools

Online benchmarking tools leverage sophisticated algorithms to analyze vast amounts of data, providing a comprehensive picture:

- **Website Analytics**: Go beyond basic traffic metrics to understand user behavior, engagement levels, and content performance on your website compared to competitors.
- **Social Media Listening**: Track online conversations across platforms, gauge brand sentiment towards your and competitor brands, and identify key influencers.
- **Search Engine Ranking Analysis**: See how your website and competitor websites rank for relevant keywords in search engines, providing insights into online visibility.

Metrics for Effective Online Benchmarking

- **Website Traffic and Engagement**: Compare website traffic volume, bounce rates, average session duration, and user behavior across different platforms (yours vs. competitors).
- **Social Media Performance**: Analyze follower growth, engagement rates (likes, comments, shares) on social media posts, and brand sentiment compared to competitors.
- **Search Engine Visibility**: Track your and your competitors' ranking for relevant keywords in search engines and the effectiveness of your content marketing strategy in driving organic traffic.
- **Brand Sentiment Analysis**: Identify the overall perception of your brand and competitor brands in online conversations, gauging patient and HCP trust, satisfaction, and brand awareness.

Benefits of Online Benchmarking

- **Identify Strengths and Weaknesses**: Benchmarking reveals areas where your online presence excels and where competitors might be performing better.

- **Optimize Your Online Strategy**: Data insights inform improvements to your website, social media engagement, content marketing, and overall digital communication strategy.
- **Improve Brand Perception**: Addressing weaknesses identified through benchmarking can enhance your online reputation and build a stronger brand image.

Examples of Online Benchmarking Strategies

- A pharmaceutical company benchmarks its website and discovers that a competitor offers a more user-friendly experience and clearer patient education resources. This prompts the company to revamp its website design and content to improve user experience and information accessibility.
- Social media listening reveals negative sentiment towards a competitor's brand due to a recent controversy. The company can develop a social media campaign highlighting its commitment to transparency and ethical practices.
- Benchmarking search engine rankings show a competitor ranking higher for key terms related to a new treatment area. This can inform the company's content marketing strategy, focusing on creating informative and SEO-optimized content to improve search engine visibility.

In conclusion, benchmarking your brand against competitors online is essential for success in the digital age. By leveraging online benchmarking tools and analyzing key metrics, pharmaceutical companies gain valuable insights to optimize their online presence, strengthen their brand image, and stay ahead of the competition.

6.2 Identifying Areas for Improvement Based on Competitor Sentiment Analysis

Staying ahead of the competition in the pharmaceutical industry requires constant innovation and improvement. Analyzing competitor sentiment online provides a treasure trove of information to identify areas where your brand can excel. Here is how:

Understanding Competitor Perception

Competitor sentiment analysis involves analyzing online conversations to understand how patients and healthcare professionals (HCPs) perceive your competitors and their products:

- **Social media discussions**: Patients share their experiences with competitor medications, treatment approaches, and marketing campaigns.
- **Online reviews**: Reviews of competitor medications offer insights into patient satisfaction, side effects, and areas for improvement.
- **Industry forums and news articles**: HCPs discuss competitor products, their effectiveness, and potential drawbacks in online forums and comment sections of news articles.

Identifying Areas for Improvement

By analyzing this online chatter, you can uncover weaknesses in your competitor's approach:

- **Patient Dissatisfaction**: If patients express frustration with a competitor's medication (e.g., side effects, complex dosing), this highlights an opportunity for your brand to develop a more patient-friendly solution.
    - **Example**: Sentiment analysis reveals widespread complaints about a competitor's diabetes medication causing fatigue as a side effect. Your company can focus on developing a medication with a lower fatigue risk, addressing this specific patient concern.

- **Marketing Gaps**: If competitor marketing campaigns are met with negative sentiment (e.g., misleading claims, lack of transparency), you can develop more ethical and informative messaging for your brand.
    - **Example**: Sentiment analysis shows negative online discussions about a competitor's marketing campaign for a new medication due to exaggerated claims of its effectiveness. Your brand can focus on promoting your medication based on scientific data and real-world patient benefits.
- **HCP Concerns**: If HCPs express concerns about a competitor's product (e.g., limited efficacy data, safety issues), you can leverage this information to address those concerns in product development and communication with HCPs.
    - **Example**: Sentiment analysis reveals HCPs questioning the long-term safety of a competitor's medicaiton; your company can prioritize conducting thorough safety studies and communicating those results to build trust with HCPs.

Turning Insights into Action

By identifying areas for improvement based on competitor sentiment analysis, you can take strategic action:

- **Product Development**: Focus research and development efforts on addressing shortcomings identified in competitor products.
- **Marketing Strategy**: Develop marketing campaigns highlighting your brand's strengths compared to the competition and address patient and HCP concerns raised online.
- **Patient Education**: Create educational materials that address patients' questions and anxieties regarding competitor medications.

Benefits of Competitor Sentiment Analysis

- **Proactive Improvement**: Identify potential weaknesses in competitor offerings before they become major issues for your brand.
- **Patient-Centric Approach**: Focus development efforts on creating solutions that address real-world patient needs and concerns identified through competitor analysis.
- **Building Brand Differentiation**: Leverage competitor shortcomings to position your brand as a more effective, ethical, and patient-centric option.

Examples of Taking Action

- A pharmaceutical company analyzes online discussions about a competitor's medication for a chronic condition and discovers that patients struggle with managing a complex dosing schedule. The company develops a new medication with a simpler and more convenient dosing regimen and emphasizes this advantage in its marketing materials.
- Sentiment analysis reveals that HCPs hesitate to prescribe a competitor's new medication because long-term efficacy data is lacking. The company prioritizes conducting and publishing comprehensive clinical trials demonstrating the medication's long-term effectiveness.

In conclusion, competitor sentiment analysis is a powerful tool for identifying areas for improvement in your brand strategy. By understanding how patients and HCPs perceive your competitors, you can develop a winning approach that addresses unmet needs, builds trust with your target audience, and positions your brand for success in the competitive pharmaceutical landscape.

6.3 Case Study: A Pharma Company Using Sentiment Analysis to Gain Insights into Competitor Marketing Strategies

The Scenario

Zenith Pharmaceuticals, a mid-sized company specializing in respiratory illness treatment, faces increasing competition from larger players in the market. To develop a more effective approach, Zenith wants to gain insights into competitor marketing strategies and identify potential weaknesses.

The Challenge

Traditionally, Zenith relied on limited methods to understand competitor marketing:

- **Competitor website monitoring**: Provides basic information but needs more insights into audience perceptions.
- **Industry Reports**: Offer broad market trends but lack specific details on competitor campaigns.
- **Limited Market Research**: Expensive and time-consuming, offering a snapshot of competitor activity.

The Solution: Sentiment Analysis

Zenith decides to leverage sentiment analysis to gain a deeper understanding of competitor marketing strategies:

- **Social media listening**: Monitor online conversations surrounding social media campaigns launched by competitor brands. This will reveal the real-time public perception of competitor messaging.
- **News article analysis**: Analyze comments on news articles discussing competitor medications and marketing initiatives. This reveals HCP (healthcare professional) perspectives on competitor strategies.

- **Patient forum insights**: Analyze discussions on patient forums where patients share their experiences with competitor medications and marketing messages.

Unveiling Competitor Strategies

By analyzing online conversations, Zenith uncovers valuable insights:

- **Messaging Focus**: They discover a competitor brand heavily focuses on celebrity endorsements in their marketing campaign, which some patients find inauthentic.
- **Content Gaps**: Sentiment analysis reveals patients lack information about the long-term side effects of a competitor's medication, a topic not addressed in their marketing materials.
- **HCP Targeting**: Competitor marketing materials seem primarily focused on general practitioners, neglecting the role of respiratory therapists in treatment decisions.

Developing a Winning Strategy

Armed with these insights, Zenith refines its marketing approach:

- **Focus on Patient Education**: Zenith develops patient-centric campaigns that address long-term side effects and provide clear information about their medicaiton.
- **Authentic Patient Testimonials**: They leverage testimonials from real patients who have benefited from their medication, fostering trust and reliability..
- **Targeted Content for HCPs**: Zenith creates educational content for respiratory therapists, highlighting their medication's role in a comprehensive treatment plan.

Measuring Success

Zenith continues to monitor online conversations to gauge the impact of their marketing strategy:

- **Increased Patient Engagement**: They observe a rise in positive online comments about the informative and transparent nature of their marketing messages.

- **Improved HCP Perception**: Sentiment analysis reveals a more positive outlook from HCPs toward Zenith's medication and their approach to educating patients and healthcare professionals.
- **Market Share Growth**: Zenith's market share gradually increases, demonstrating the effectiveness of its data-driven marketing strategy.

Lessons Learned

This case study highlights the value of sentiment analysis for understanding competitor marketing strategies:

- **Unveiling Weaknesses**: This will allow you to identify potential shortcomings in competitor campaigns and messaging and develop a more targeted and effective strategy.
- **Patient-Centric Approach**: Sentiment analysis helps tailor marketing materials to address real patient concerns and information gaps, fostering trust and brand loyalty.
- **Building Strong Relationships with HCPs**: Zenith understands HCP needs and preferences and creates targeted content that strengthens their relationships within the healthcare community.

In conclusion, this case study demonstrates how sentiment analysis empowers pharmaceutical companies to gain valuable insights into competitor marketing strategies. By understanding the audience's perception of competitor campaigns, companies can develop effective messaging that resonates with patients and HCPs, achieving market success.

Part III. Implementing Sentiment Analysis: A Step-by-Step Guide

Sentiment analysis can be a powerful tool for the pharmaceutical industry, but putting it into action requires specific steps. Here is a breakdown of the process:

Step 1: Define Your Goals and Target Audience

- **What do you want to achieve?** Are you analyzing patient education materials, gauging competitor marketing campaigns, or understanding patient sentiment toward your brand?
- **Who are you targeting?** Are you focusing on patients, healthcare professionals (HCPs), or both? Understanding your target audience helps you tailor your data collection and analysis.

Step 2: Data Collection

- **Identify data sources**: Social media platforms (Twitter, Facebook), online reviews, patient forums, news articles (comment sections), and industry websites are all valuable data sources.
- **Utilize data collection tools**: Many web scrapping tools and social media listening platforms can automate data collection, saving time and effort.

Step 3: Data Preprocessing

- **Cleaning the data**: Remove irrelevant information, such as punctuation symbols and stop words (common words like "the" or "and"), to ensure the analysis focuses on meaningful content.
- **Normalization**: Convert text to lowercase and address your typos or slang for consistency within the data.

Step 4: Choosing a Sentiment Analysis Technique

- **Lexicon-based approach**: This method uses predefined dictionaries or lists of words with positive, negative, or neutral sentiments.

- **Machine learning techniques**: Involve automatically training algorithms on labeled data sets to identify sentiment. This can be more nuanced than lexicon-based methods.

Step 5: Sentiment Analysis and Visualization:

- **Run the analysis**: Use your chosen sentiment analysis tool or software to categorize the collected data as positive, negative, or neutral sentiment.
- **Data Visualization**: Create charts and graphs to visualize the sentiment distribution (positive, negative, neutral) across your target audience and different groups.

Step 6: Interpretation and Action

- **Analyze the results**: Based on the sentiment analysis, identify trends, common themes, and areas of strength or weakness.
- **Take Action**: Based on your findings, refine your patient education materials, adjust your marketing strategy, or address concerns raised online.

Additional Considerations

- **Data Security**: Ensure you comply with privacy regulations when collecting and analyzing online data.
- **Human Review**: While sentiment analysis is powerful, it is not perfect. To ensure accuracy and capture context, include a human review of the data.
- **Continuous Monitoring**: Sentiment analysis is an ongoing process. Monitor online conversations regularly to stay updated on patient and HCP perceptions.

By following these steps and considering the additional points, you can implement sentiment analysis effectively to gain valuable insights and improve your brand strategy in the pharmaceutical industry.

CHAPTER

7

Defining Your Sentiment Analysis: Goals and Objectives

Sentiment analysis is a powerful tool, but like any tool, it's most effective when used with a clear purpose. This chapter focuses on the crucial first step: defining your goals and objectives for sentiment analysis within the pharmaceutical industry:

Why Define Goals Before Diving In?

- **Focus and Direction**: Clearly defined goals ensure your sentiment analysis efforts are targeted and deliver actionable insights.
- **Data Collection Strategy**: Knowing your goals helps determine the most relevant data sources and the type of data you need to collect for effective analysis.
- **Evaluation and Measurement**: Defined objectives allow you to measure the success of your sentiment analysis efforts and track progress toward your goals.

Common Goals for Sentiment Analysis in Pharma

- **Understanding Patient Needs and Concerns**: Analyze online reviews, forums, and social media discussions to identify patient anxieties, frustrations, and unmet needs regarding medications and treatment options.
  - **Example Goal**: Identify patients' top three concerns regarding a new medicaiton your company is developing.

- **Optimizing Patient Education Materials**: Analyze how patients engage with your educational resources. This will help you identify areas for improvement, ensure your materials are clear and informative, and effectively address patient questions.
  - **Example Goal**: Increase patient comprehension of medicaiton side effects by 20% through revisions based on sentiment analysis of existing educational materials.
- **Gauging Brand Perception**: Analyze online conversations to understand how patients and healthcare professionals (HCPs) perceive your brand, its reputation, and its place within the treatment landscape.
  - **Example Goal:** Increase positive sentiment toward Brand X by 15% on social media platforms through targeted marketing campaigns informed by sentiment analysis.
- **Benchmarking Against Competitors**: Analyze online conversations surrounding competitor brands and medications. This lets you identify their strengths and weaknesses, informing your product development and marketing strategies.
  - **Example Goal**: Identify areas where competitors' marketing campaigns are met with negative sentiment and develop a campaign that effectively addresses those concerns for your brand.

Developing SMART Objectives

S.M.A.R.T. stands for Specific, Measurable, Achievable, Relevant, and Time-bound. When defining your sentiment analysis objectives, ensure they are:

- **Specific**: Clearly state what you want to achieve (e.g., increase patient satisfaction by 10%).
- **Measurable**: Define metrics to track progress toward your objective (e.g., positive sentiment mentions in online reviews).

- **Achievable**: Set realistic goals that can be reached within a specific timeframe.
- **Relevant**: Objectives should directly align with your overall marketing or brand strategy.
- **Time-bound**: Set a timeframe for achieving your objectives (e.g., increase website engagement by 20% within three months).

Tips for Defining Goals and Objectives

- **Align with Business Goals**: Ensure your sentiment analysis goals support your overall marketing and brand strategy for the pharmaceutical company.
- **Start Specific, Broaden Later**: Begin with a specific goal for a particular campaign or product launch. As you gain experience, you can broaden your objectives.
- **Focus on Actionable Insights**: Your goals should ultimately lead to actionable strategies that improve communication, brand perception, or patient education.

By clearly defining your goals and objectives for sentiment analysis, you set the stage for a successful journey. With a targeted approach, you can leverage the power of sentiment analysis to gain valuable insights, improve your brand strategy, and achieve your goals in the competitive pharmaceutical industry.

7.1 What Do You Want to Achieve with Sentiment Analysis?

In the world of pharmaceuticals, sentiment analysis can be a powerful tool to achieve various goals. Here are some key objectives companies might aim for:

1. **Understanding Patient Needs and Concerns**:
   - By analyzing online reviews, forums, and social media discussions, companies can identify what patients are worried or confused about regarding medications and treatments. This can help them address those concerns in educational materials or future product development.
   - **Example Goal**: A company might use sentiment analysis to identify the top 3 medication side effects patients are most anxious about.
2. **Optimizing Patient Education Materials:**
   - Sentiment analysis can help assess how patients interact with the company's educational resources. This can reveal areas for improvement, ensuring the materials are clear and informative and effectively address patient questions.
   - **Example Goal**: A company might aim to increase patient comprehension of medication side effects by 20% through revisions based on sentiment analysis of existing brochures.
3. **Gauging Brand Perception**:
   - Analyzing online conversations can provide insights into how patients and healthcare professionals (HCPs) view the brand, its reputation, and its place within the treatment landscape.
   - **Example Goal**: A company might target increasing positive sentiment towards its brand by 15% on social media platforms through targeted marketing campaigns informed by sentiment analysis.

4. **Benchmarking Against Competitors**:
   - Analyzing online conversations surrounding competitor brands and medications allows companies to identify their strengths and weaknesses, which can inform their product development and marketing strategies.
   - **Example Goal**: A company might aim to identify areas where competitors' marketing campaigns are met with negative sentiment and develop a campaign that effectively addresses those concerns for their brand.

Overall, sentiment analysis helps companies gather valuable insights from vast online conversations. By understanding what people say and feel, pharmaceutical companies can make data-driven decisions to improve communication, brand perception, and patient education, leading to their success in the marketplace.

7.2 Aligning Your Sentiment Analysis Plan with Your Overall Marketing and Communication Strategies

Aligning your sentiment analysis plan with your overall marketing and communication strategies involves ensuring your analysis efforts directly support your brand's messaging and goals. Here is how to achieve this alignment:

1. **Understanding Your Marketing and Communication Goals**:
   - **Start with the Big Picture**: Before diving into sentiment analysis, clearly define your overall marketing and communication goals. Are you aiming to launch a new product, increase brand awareness, or improve patient education?
   - **Identify Target Audience**: Who are you trying to reach with your marketing and communication efforts? Understanding your target audience (patients, HCPs, both) is crucial for directing your sentiment analysis.
2. **Tailoring Sentiment Analysis to Your Goals**:
   - **Targeted Data Collection**: Choose relevant data sources for sentiment analysis based on your goals. For example, analyzing patient forums might be ideal for understanding medicaiton concerns, while social media listening could reveal brand perception among a broader audience.
   - **Focus on Actionable Insights**: Don't get lost in the data! Ensure your sentiment analysis helps answer specific questions relevant to your marketing and communication goals.
   - **Example**: If your goal is to improve patient education, analyze online reviews to identify confusion regarding medication instructions.

3. **Integrating Insights into Strategy**:
   - **Inform Marketing Campaigns**: Use sentiment analysis to tailor your marketing messages. Address patient concerns identified online, highlight your brand's strengths compared to competitors, and develop messaging that resonates with your target audience.
   - **Enhance Communication Materials**: Sentiment analysis can help improve patient education materials, website content, and FAQs. Ensure your communication is clear and informative and addresses the questions and needs revealed through online analysis.

Examples of Alignment:

- A pharmaceutical company launching a new medication for diabetes uses sentiment analysis to understand patient concerns about existing medication (e.g., side effects, complex dosing). Their marketing campaign emphasizes the new medication's convenience and reduced side effects.
- Sentiment analysis reveals that a brand is not trusted due to a recent controversy. The company uses this insight to develop a communication strategy focused on transparency and ethical practices, rebuilding trust with patients and HCPs.

Benefits of Alignment:

- **Focused Efforts**: Aligning sentiment analysis with your overall strategy ensures your efforts are targeted and deliver actionable insights.
- **Data-Driven Decisions**: Real-world data from online conversations can inform your marketing and communication strategies, leading to more effective campaigns and improved brand perception.
- **Meeting Patient Needs**: By understanding patient concerns and information gaps revealed through sentiment analysis,

your communication can be more patient-centric, fostering trust and loyalty.

In conclusion, aligning your sentiment analysis plan with your marketing communication strategies is crucial for maximizing the value of this powerful tool. By understanding your audience, tailoring your analysis, and integrating insights into your overall strategy, you can leverage sentiment analysis to achieve your brand's marketing and communication goals.

CHAPTER 8

Selecting the Right Tools and Data Sources

Sentiment analysis offers many pharmaceutical insights, but success hinges on choosing the right tools and data sources. This chapter equips you to build a solid foundation for your sentiment analysis journey.

Choosing the Right Tools

The best sentiment analysis tool depends on your specific needs and budget. Here are the key factors to consider:

- **Features and Functionality**: Different tools offer varying capabilities. Some provide basic sentiment analysis (positive, negative, neutral), while others offer more advanced features like topic modeling or identifying emotions (anger, joy, etc.).
- **Ease of Use**: Consider the technical expertise within your team. Some tools require programming knowledge, while others offer user-friendly interfaces.
- **Cost**: Sentiment analysis tools range from free, open-source options to enterprise-grade solutions with subscription fees.

Examples of Sentiment Analysis Tools:

- **Free/Open-Source Tools**: Apache OpenNLP, TextBlob
- **Paid Subscription Tools**: Brandwatch Analytics, Sprout Social, Lexalytics

Choosing the Right Data Sources:

The quality and relevance of your data significantly impact the insights you gain. Here are some valuable data sources for sentiment analysis in pharma:

- **Social Media Platforms**: Twitter (X now), Facebook, and patient advocacy group forums offer real-time conversations between patients and HCPs about medications, treatments, and brands.
- **Online Review Sites**: Review platforms dedicated to medications or healthcare providers offer patient perspectives on medication effectiveness, side effects, and overall experience.
- **Industry Websites and News Articles**: Analyze comment sections of news articles discussing new medications or industry trends to understand HCP and public perception.
- **Patient Forums and Support Groups**: Online forums allow patients to share experiences, ask questions, and express anxiety about medications and treatment options.
- **Company Websites and Customer Reviews**: Analyze reviews and comments on your website to identify areas for improvement in communication and patient education materials.

Considerations for Data Source Selection:

- **Relevance to Your Goals**: Align your data sources with specific sentiment analysis objectives.
    - **Example**: To understand patient education needs, analyze online reviews and patient forum discussions.
- **Data Quality and Credibility**: Be cautious of unreliable sources or biased information. When collecting data, consider the reputation of the website or forum.
- **Data Privacy Regulations**: Ensure compliance with data privacy regulations when collecting and analyzing online data.

Building a Robust Data Collection Strategy:

- **Combine Data Sources**: Don't rely on a single source. Utilize various data sources to gain a more comprehensive understanding of sentiment.
- **Utilize Data Collection Tools**: Many web scraping tools and social media listening platforms automate data collection, saving time and effort.
- **Regular Data Monitoring:** Sentiment analysis is an ongoing process. Monitor online conversations regularly to stay updated on patient and HCP perceptions.

By carefully selecting the right tools and data sources, you lay the groundwork for successful sentiment analysis in the pharmaceutical industry. With a robust data collection strategy, you can gather valuable insights to inform your brand strategy and communication efforts and improve patient care.

8.1 Exploring Different Sentiment Analysis Tools and Platforms

In the pharmaceutical Industry, sentiment analysis can be a game changer. But to harness its power, you need the right tools. This section explores various sentiment analysis tools and platforms available, helping you choose the one that best suits your needs.

Types of Sentiment Analysis Tools

- **Lexicon-Based Tools**: These workhorses categorize text based on predefined lists of positive, negative, and neutral words. They offer a simple and fast approach but might miss sarcasm or nuanced language.
    - **Examples**: TextBlob (open-source), SentiWordNet (open-source)
- **Machine Learning**: These advanced tools are trained on vast amounts of labeled data, allowing them to identify sentiment with greater accuracy and capture more subtle emotions.
    - **Examples**: Brandwatch Analytics, Sprout Social, Amazon Comprehend
- **Hybrid Tools** combine lexicon-based and machine-learning approaches, balancing ease of use and accuracy.
    - **Example**: Synthesio, Google Cloud Natural Language API

Factors to Consider When Choosing a Tool

- **Features and Functionality**: Make a list of your needs. Do you need basic sentiment analysis (positive/negative/neutral) or advanced features like topic modeling or emotion detection?
- **Data Source Integration**: Ensure the tool integrates with the data sources you plan to use (e.g., social media platforms, online review sites). Not all tools support all data sources.
- **Ease of Use**: Consider your team's technical expertise. Some tools require programming knowledge, while others offer user-friendly interfaces with drag-and-drop functionalities.

- **Cost**: Sentiment analysis tools range from free, open-source options to enterprise-grade solutions with subscription fees. Determine your budget and find a tool that offers your desired features within your price range.

Exploring Popular Sentiment Analysis Tools

Here is a glimpse into some popular sentiment analysis tools, categorized based on their approach:

- **Free / Open-Source Lexicon-Based Tools**:
  - **Apache OpenNLP**: A powerful and versatile open-source toolkit for natural language processing (NLP) tasks, including sentiment analysis. Requires programming knowledge.
  - **TextBlob**: A Python library offering a simple and user-friendly API for sentiment analysis. Great for beginners or quick sentiment checks.
- **Paid Subscription – Machine Learning Tools**:
  - **Brandwatch Analytics**: A comprehensive social listening platform offering sentiment analysis, brand reputation monitoring, and competitor benchmarking.
  - **Sprout Social**: A social media management platform with built-in sentiment analysis features to track audience perception across various social media channels.
  - **Lexalytics Semantria**: An enterprise-grade solution offering advanced sentiment analysis capabilities, including topic modeling and entity extraction.
- **Paid Subscription – Hybrid Tools**:
  - **Synthesio**: A social listening platform that combines machine learning and human expertise for in-depth sentiment analysis and social media insights.
  - **Google Cloud Natural Language API**: A cloud-based API offering various NLP features, including sentiment analysis with customizable options.

Additional Considerations

- **Free Trials**: Many paid tools offer free trials, allowing you to test-drive their feature before committing.
- **Industry-Specific Solutions**: Some companies offer sentiment analysis tools specifically tailored to the pharmaceutical industry, with pre-built features and industry-specific lexicons.
- **Security and Privacy**: When handling patient-related data, ensure the tool adheres to data privacy regulations (e.g., GDPR, HIPAA).

Remember, the "best" tool depends on your needs and budget. By considering the factors mentioned above and exploring the available options, you can choose the sentiment analysis tool that empowers you to gain valuable insights from online conversations and improve your brand strategy in the pharmaceutical industry.

8.2 Identifying Relevant Data Sources For Your Analysis: Social Media, Online Reviews, Forums, etc.

Sentiment analysis is a powerful tool in pharmaceuticals, but its effectiveness hinges on the quality and relevance of the data. This section explores the best data sources for your specific sentiment analysis needs within the pharmaceutical industry.

Treasure Trove of Online Conversations

The pharmaceutical industry can leverage a wealth of online conversations to understand patient needs, brand perception, and competitor strategies. Here are some key data sources to consider:

A. **Social Media Platforms:**

- **Twitter (X now)**: A real-time platform for patient discussions about medications, side effects, and treatment experiences. Hashtags can help track specific conversations.
- **Facebook Groups**: Patient advocacy groups and disease-specific communities offer insights into patient anxieties, treatment journeys, and brand preferences.
- **YouTube Comments**: Analyze comments on videos discussing medications or healthcare topics to understand patient concerns and information gaps.

B. **Online Review Sites:**

- **WebMD Reviews**: A platform dedicated to mediation reviews, offering valuable patient perspectives on effectiveness, side effects, and ease of use.
- **drugs.com Reviews**: Another popular platform for medication reviews, often including user ratings and comparisons between different medications.
- **Healthcare Provider Review Sites**: Sites like Healthgrades or Zocdoc allow patients to review their experiences with doctors and hospitals, potentially revealing

insights into the brand perception of medications prescribed.

C. **Forums and Support Groups:**

- **Disease-Specific Forums**: Online forums dedicated to specific conditions can provide in-depth discussions about treatment options, medication experiences, and emotional aspects of living with a certain illness.
- **Pharmaceutical Company Forums**: Many pharmaceutical companies host online forums where patients can ask questions and share experiences with medications produced by the company.

D. **Industry Websites and News Articles:**

- **News Comment Sections**: Analyze comments on news articles discussing new medications, clinical trials, or industry trends to understand public perception and potential concerns.
- **Medical News Websites**: Websites like Medscape or WebMD often feature comment sections where healthcare professionals (HCPs) can share their perspectives on new medications or treatment approaches.

Choosing the Right Sources for Your Goals

Not all data sources are created equal. Here is how to pick the most relevant ones for your sentiment analysis goals:

- **Understanding Patient Needs**: Focus on online reviews, patient forums, and social media discussions about medications and treatment experiences.
- **Gauging Brand Perception**: Analyze social media conversations, online reviews, and potential news comment sections to understand overall brand perception among patients and the public.

- **Benchmarking Against Competitors**: Social media listening tools can track conversations surrounding competitor brands and medications, revealing their strengths and weaknesses.
- **Optimizing Patient Education Materials**: Analyze reviews of existing educational materials on your company website or patient forums to identify areas for improvement.

Additional Considerations

- **Data Quality**: Be cautious of unreliable sources or biased information. When collecting data, consider the reputation of the website or forum.
- **Data Privacy**: When collecting and analyzing data, especially patient-related information, ensure compliance with data privacy regulations (e.g., GDPR, HIPAA).
- **Data Security**: Choose data collection tools that prioritize data security to protect patient privacy.

By identifying the right data sources and considering these additional factors, you can ensure that your sentiment analysis is based on relevant and reliable information. This will empower you to extract valuable insights for improving your brand strategy, communication efforts, and patient care in the pharmaceutical industry.

8.3 Setting up Data Collection and Analysis Processes

In the world of pharmaceuticals, sentiment analysis can be a game-changer. But to translate potential into reality, you need a well-defined data collection and analysis process. This section equips you to set up a system that delivers valuable insights for your brand.

Building Your Data Collection Process

1. **Identify Data Sources**: Refer to the previous section on identifying relevant sources, such as social media platforms, online review sites, and patient forums. Align these sources with your specific sentiment analysis goals.
2. **Choose Data Collection Tools:** Several tools can automate data collection, saving time and effort. Here are some options:
   - **Social media listening platforms**: These tools track conversations on various social media channels and allow you to filter data by keywords or hashtags (e.g., Brandwatch, Sprout Social).
   - **Web scraping tools**: Extract data from specific websites, allowing you to collect reviews, forum discussions, or comments (Use with caution and comply with website terms of service).
   - **APIs**: Some data sources offer Application Programming Interfaces (APIs) that allow you to collect data (e.g., Twitter API) programmatically.
3. **Set Up Data Collection Parameters:**
   - **Keywords and Hashtags**: Define keywords and hashtags relevant to your analysis. For example, if analyzing patient sentiment toward a new medication, include the medication name, brand name, and potential side effects as keywords.
   - **Date Range**: Determine the time frame for data collection. Consider how far back you need data to understand current sentiment or track trends over time.

- **Data Filtering**: Set filters to exclude irrelevant information. For example, you should exclude spam or bot accounts on social media.

4. **Schedule Regular Data Collection:**
    - **Real-Time vs. Historical Data**: Real-time data collection might be crucial for some goals (e.g., gauging brand perception during a new marketing campaign launch). For others (e.g., understanding long-term patient experiences with a medicaiton), historical data might be more valuable.
    - **Schedule Automation:** Many data collection tools allow you to schedule automated data collection at regular intervals, ensuring a steady stream of fresh data for analysis.

Data Analysis Workflow:

1. **Data Cleaning and Preprocessing:**
    - **Remove irrelevant information**: Clean your data by removing punctuation, symbols, and stop words (common words like "the" or "and") to focus on meaningful content.
    - **Normalize the data**: To ensure consistency within the data set, convert text to lowercase and address typos or slang.
2. **Choose a Sentiment Analysis Technique:**
    - **Lexicon-based approach**: This method uses predefined dictionaries or lists of words with positive, negative, or neutral sentiment. It's a simple approach but might miss nuanced language.
    - **Machine learning techniques**: Involve training algorithms on labeled data sets to identify sentiment and capture more subtle emotions more accurately. These techniques are generally more powerful but require more technical expertise.
3. **Sentiment Analysis and Visualization:**
    - **Run the analysis**: Use your chosen sentiment analysis tool or software to categorize the collected data as positive, negative, or neutral sentiment.

  - **Data Visualization**: Create charts and graphs to visualize the sentiment distribution (positive, negative, neutral) across different topics, medications, or brands.

4. **Interpretation and Action**:
   - **Analyze the results**: Based on the sentiment analysis, identify trends, common themes, and areas of strength or weakness. Look for positive and negative sentiment patterns and topics that trigger stronger emotions.
   - **Take Action**: Based on your findings, refine your patient education materials, adjust your marketing strategy, or address concerns raised online.

Additional Considerations:

- **Data Security**: Ensure you have proper security measures to protect patient data collected during the analysis process.
- **Human Review**: While sentiment analysis tools are powerful, they are not perfect. Include a human review of the data to ensure accuracy and capture context that machines might miss.
- **Continuous Monitoring**: Sentiment analysis is an ongoing process. Monitor online conversations regularly to stay updated on patient and HCP perceptions.

Establishing a well-defined data collection and analysis process can ensure that your sentiment analysis efforts are efficient and reliable. This process can also deliver actionable insights to empower your brand strategy and improve patient care in the pharmaceutical industry.

CHAPTER

9

Extracting Insights from the Data: Actionable Strategies

In the pharmaceutical industry, sentiment analysis is more than collecting data; it's about transforming it into actionable insights that drive positive change. This chapter explains how to analyze sentiment analysis results and translate them into concrete strategies for your brand.

From Data to Insights: A Closer Look

After running your sentiment analysis, you will have a wealth of data categorized as positive, negative, or neutral sentiment. But the key lies in interpreting this data and uncovering the underlying stories. Here's how to approach this:

- **Identify Trends**: Look for patterns in sentiment distribution across different topics, medications, or brands. Are there specific areas generating primarily positive or negative sentiment?
- **Theme Detection**: Analyze the content associated with positive and negative sentiment. What topics or concerns are patients frequently mentioning? Are there recurring themes across different data sources?
- **Comparative Analysis**: If your analysis included competitor brands, compare the sentiment towards your brand and theirs. Identify areas where you outperform competitors and areas for improvement.

Turning Insights into Action:

Now that you have valuable insights, it's time to translate them into actionable strategies for your brand:

- **Optimizing Patient Education**: Sentiment analysis can reveal areas for improvement in your patient education materials:
  - **Example**: If analysis shows confusion regarding medication dosage, revise your brochures or website content to provide clearer instructions.
- **Enhancing Marketing and Communication**: Use sentiment analysis to inform your marketing messages and communication strategies.
  - **Example**: If patients express anxiety about side effects, develop marketing materials that address those concerns and highlight the medication's benefits.
- **Improving Patient Experience**: Sentiment analysis can help identify areas where the patient experience can be improved.
  - **Example**: If online reviews reveal long wait times at clinics where your medication is prescribed, work with healthcare providers to address the issue.

Developing Actionable Insights

Here are some additional tips for translating insights into action:

- **Focus on Specific and Measurable Goals**: Don't get overwhelmed by the data. Set specific and measurable goals based on your insights.
  - **Example Goal**: Increase patient comprehension of medication side effects by 20% through revisions based on sentiment analysis.
- **Develop a Clear Action Plan**: Outline a plan for implementing your strategies. Define timelines, responsibilities, and resources needed to achieve your goals.
- **Track Progress and Measure Results**: Monitor the impact

of your strategies regularly. Use sentiment analysis to track changes in patient sentiment over time.

Examples of Actionable Insights

- A pharmaceutical company uses sentiment analysis to identify patient concerns about the affordability of their medication. The company develops a patient assistance program to address and communicate this concern through targeted marketing campaigns.
- Sentiment analysis reveals that a competitor's brand is criticized for lacking transparency. A company leverages this insight to develop a marketing campaign emphasizing its commitment to open communication and patient education.

Remember, sentiment analysis is a powerful tool, but it's just one piece of the puzzle. Combine your data-driven insights with your market and brand strategy understanding to develop effective action plans.

By following these steps and focusing on actionable strategies, you can transform the data from sentiment analysis into tangible improvements for your brand. This will improve patient care and your position in the competitive pharmaceutical industry.

9.1 Analyzing Sentiment Data and Identifying Key Trends and Patterns

When it comes to sentiment analysis in the pharmaceutical industry, it's all about sifting through a mountain of online conversations and reviews to find the nuggets of gold — the key trends and patterns that can inform your brand strategy. Here's how you can do that:

Unpacking Your Data

After running your sentiment analysis, you'll have a dataset categorized as positive, negative, or neutral sentiment. But that's just the starting point. Now comes the detective work!

- **Look for Trends**: Imagine the data as a landscape. Are there areas with mostly positive sentiment, like discussions about a medication's effectiveness? Or are there valleys of negativity, perhaps focused on side effects? Look for patterns in how sentiment is distributed across different topics, brands, or medications.
- **Theme Detective**: Dive Deeper! Analyze the content associated with both positive and negative sentiment. What are people talking about? Are recurring themes or concerns popping up across different sources like social media and online reviews?
  - **Example**: Positive sentiment revolves around a medication's ease of use, while negative sentiment mentions frequent headaches as a side effect.
- **Comparative Analysis (Optional)**: If you include competitor brands in your analysis, it gets interesting. Compare the sentiment toward your brand and theirs. Are there areas where you shine and they struggle? Identifying these areas of strength and weakness can be a goldmine for strategic decision-making.

From Trends to Strategies

Once you have identified these trends and patterns, it's time to take action! Here's how to turn those insights into improvements for your brand.

- **Optimizing Patient Education**: Sentiment analysis can reveal gaps in your patient education materials.
  - **Example**: Did the analysis show confusion regarding medication dosing? Revise your brochures or website content to provide clearer instructions.
- **Enhancing Marketing and Communication**: Use sentiment analysis to inform your marketing messages and communication strategies.
  - **Example**: If patients express anxiety about side effects, develop marketing materials that address those concerns and highlight the medication's benefits.
- **Improving Patient Experience**: Sentiment analysis can help identify areas where the patient experience can be improved.
  - **Example**: Do online reviews reveal long wait times at clinics prescribing your medication? Use this insight to work with healthcare providers to address the issue.

Tips for Turning Insights into Action

- **Focus and Measure**: Don't get lost in the data. Set specific and measurable goals based on your insights.
  - **Example Goal**: Increase patient comprehension of medication side effects by 20% through revisions based on sentiment analysis.
- **Action Plan**: Develop a clear plan for implementing your strategies. Define timelines, responsibilities, and resources needed to achieve your goals.
- **Track Progress**: Regularly monitor the impact of your strategies. Use sentiment analysis to track changes in patient

sentiment over time. This helps you measure success and identify areas for further improvement.

Remember, sentiment analysis is a tool, not a magic solution. Combine your data-driven insights with your market and brand strategy understanding to develop effective action plans.

By following these steps and focusing on trends and patterns, you can transform the data from sentiment analysis into tangible improvements for your brand. This will lead to better patient care and a stronger position in the pharmaceutical industry.

9.2 Utilizing Data Visualization Tools to Effectively Communicate Insights

Sentiment analysis offers a wealth of insights into pharmaceuticals, but translating those insights into action requires clear communication. Data visualization tools come to the rescue! They help you transform complex data sets into charts, graphs, and other visuals that effectively communicate the key trends and patterns you have identified through sentiment analysis.

The Power of Visuals

- **Enhanced Understanding**: Visualizations make complex data sets easier for technical and non-technical audiences to understand. A well-designed chart can reveal patterns and trends that might be missed in raw data tables.
- **Improved Communication**: Data visualizations are powerful communication tools. They can be used in presentations, reports, and meetings to convey your findings effectively to colleagues, stakeholders, and even patients (depending on the complexity).
- **Focused Discussion**: Visuals can guide discussions and focus attention on specific aspects of your sentiment analysis. Charts can highlight areas of strength or weakness, prompting further analysis or strategic decision-making.

Choosing the Right Visualization Tool

Various data visualization tools are available, some simple and some more complex. Here are some factors to consider when choosing a tool:

- **Ease of Use**: Select a tool that aligns with your technical expertise. Some tools offer drag-and-drop functionality, while others require programming knowledge.

- **Features**: Consider the types of visualizations you need to create. Common options include bar charts, line charts, pie charts, and heat maps. Some tools offer more advanced features, such as interactive elements or the ability to create custom visualizations.
- **Data Integration**: Ensure the tool integrates with your data analysis software or spreadsheets where your sentiment analysis results are stored.

Popular Data Visualization Tools

Here are some popular data visualization tools, categorized based on their complexity:

- **Simple and User-Friendly**:
  - **Microsoft Excel**: Yes, Excel offers basic charting functionalities for creating bar charts, line charts, and pie charts to present your sentiment analysis findings.
  - **Google Sheets**: Similar to Excel, Google Sheets offers basic charting options suitable for creating clear and concise data visualizations.
- **More Features and Customization:**
  - **Tableau**: A powerful and versatile tool offering a wide range of chart types, customization options, and dashboards for presenting your sentiment analysis results.
  - **Power BI**: Another popular choice, Power BI from Microsoft, offers a user-friendly interface for creating interactive data visualization and reports.

Creating Effective Visualizations for Sentiment Analysis

- **Focus on Clarity**: Keep your visualizations clear and uncluttered. Avoid overloading your charts with too much information or using excessive colors and fonts.
- **Context is Key**: Provide context for your visualizations. Include labels, titles, and legends to ensure viewers understand the data.

- **Highlight Key Trends**: Use visuals to highlight the key trends and patterns you identified in your sentiment analysis. Annotations or call-to-action elements can further emphasize your message.

Utilizing Visualizations in Communication

- **Tailor Your Audience**: Consider your audience's technical background when visualizing your data. Use simpler charts for non-technical audiences and more complex visualizations for those familiar with data analysis.
- **Tell a Story**: Use your data visualizations to tell a story about the insights you gained from sentiment analysis. Explain what the data reveals and how it can inform your brand strategy or communication efforts.
- **Encourage Questions**: Data visualizations are a springboard for discussion. Encourage questions and feedback from your audience to ensure a clear understanding and effective communication of your sentiment analysis findings.

By effectively leveraging data visualization tools, you can transform complex data sets into impactful visuals that communicate valuable insights from your sentiment analysis in the pharmaceutical industry. This will empower you to make data-driven decisions, improve stakeholder communication, and contribute to better patient care.

9.3 Deriving Actionable Strategies Based on Your Sentiment Analysis Findings

Sentiment analysis provides valuable insights into pharmaceuticals. However, it is best to translate those insights into actionable strategies to unlock its value. This section equips you to take the findings from your analysis and develop concrete plans to improve your brand and patient experience.

From Insights to Action: A Strategic Approach

After analyzing your sentiment data, you'll have a wealth of information about perceptions, brand image, and areas for improvement. Here's how to bridge the gap and develop actionable strategies:

1. **Identify Areas of Focus**: Based on your analysis, pinpoint the key areas requiring attention. This might involve:
   - **Addressing Patient Concerns**: Are there recurring themes of anxiety about side effects, confusion regarding medication use, or dissatisfaction with treatment options?
   - **Encourage Brand Perception**: Does sentiment analysis reveal a need to improve brand trust, transparency, or communication with patients and healthcare professionals (HCPs)?
   - **Optimizing Patient Education Materials**: Do online reviews highlight areas for improvement in the clarity or comprehensiveness of your educational brochures or website content?
2. **Set SMART Goals**: Avoid generalities. Instead, define specific, Measurable, Achievable, Relevant, and Time-bound (SMART) goals based on your chosen focus area.
   - **Example**: Increase patient comprehension of medication dosage by 20% within six months through revisions to educational materials informed by sentiment analysis.

3. **Develop Action Plans**: It's time to translate your goals into concrete steps. Each action plan should outline the following:
   - **Activities**: Define the specific activities required to achieve your goal. This might involve revising educational materials, developing targeted marketing campaigns, or collaborating with HCPs to address patient concerns.
   - **Resources**: Identify the resources needed for each activity. This could include personnel, budget allocation, or access to specific data or technology.
   - **Timeline**: Set a realistic timeline for each activity and the overall action plan.
4. **Prioritization**: Not all strategies are equal. Prioritize your action plans based on urgency and potential impact. Address critical issues first and consider the available resources.

Examples of Actionable Strategies

- **Addressing Patient Concerns**: If sentiment analysis reveals anxiety about side effects, develop a patient education campaign that explains potential side effects and mitigation strategies. Partner with HCPs to ensure they are well-equipped to address patient questions and concerns.
- **Enhancing Brand Perception**: If trust is an issue, implement a communication strategy focused on transparency. Regularly share information about ongoing research, clinical trials, and potential benefits and drawbacks of your medications.
- **Optimizing Patient Education Materials**: Based on sentiment analysis of online reviews, revise your educational brochures or website content to address areas of confusion regarding medication use or potential side effects. Ensure the information is clear, concise, and easy to understand for patients.

Remember, successful strategies are:

- **Data-Driven**: Backed by the insights gleaned from your sentiment analysis.

- **Patient-Centric**: Focused on addressing patient needs and concerns and improving their experience.
- **Measurable**: This allows you to track progress and address the effectiveness of your strategy over time.

Conclusion

By following these steps and focusing on actionable strategies, you can transform the data from sentiment analysis into tangible improvements for your brand and patient care. This data-driven approach can empower you to make informed decisions, build stronger relationships with patients and HCPs, and solidify your position in the competitive pharmaceutical industry.

Part IV. The Future of Sentiment Analysis in Pharma

10. Emerging Trends and Advancements in Sentiment Analysis
11. Conclusion: The Power of Listening in Pharma Marketing

Sentiment analysis revolutionizes pharmaceutical companies' understanding of patients, brands, and market trends. But this is just the beginning. As technology advances, we can expect even more exciting developments in the future of sentiment analysis within the pharmaceutical industry.

Here are Some Key Trends to Watch:

- **Advanced NLP and AI Capabilities**: Natural Language Processing (NLP) and Artificial Intelligence (AI) constantly evolve. Future sentiment analysis tools will leverage even more sophisticated algorithms to capture the nuances of human language, including sarcasm, sentiment intensity, and emotions beyond basic positive, negative, and neutral.
- **Integration with Other Data Sources**: Sentiment analysis won't exist in a silo. Imagine integrating real-world data like prescription trends, healthcare claims data, and clinical trial results alongside social media conversations and online reviews. This holistic view will provide an even deeper understanding of patient experiences and treatment outcomes.
- **Predictive Analytics**: Sentiment analysis can become predictive in the future. By analyzing historical data and current trends, these tools might forecast future patient concerns or identify potential public perception issues surrounding upcoming drug launches.
- **Real-Time Risk Management**: Sentiment analysis can be a powerful tool for real-time risk management. By monitoring online conversations, companies can quickly identify potential safety concerns or adverse event reports, allowing for faster intervention and improved patient safety.
- **Rise of Patient-Centric Communication**: The future is about empowering patients. Sentiment analysis can inform the development of personalized communication strategies, allowing pharmaceutical companies to tailor messaging and educational materials to address different patient groups'

specific needs and concerns.

These advancements will usher in a new era of patient-centricity and data-driven decision-making in the pharmaceutical industry. Here is how this future might look:

- **Personalized Medication Education**: Imagine a future where sentiment analysis personalizes medication education. Patients would receive educational materials tailored to their questions and concerns, which would be identified through analysis of online reviews or social media conversations.
- **Proactive Patient Engagemen**t: Pharmaceutical companies can leverage sentiment analysis to engage with patients proactively. They can identify patients expressing concerns online and reach out to them directly, offering support and addressing their anxieties.
- **Real-World Evidence for Drug Development**: Sentiment analysis can play a role in real-world evidence collection and inform future drug development efforts. By understanding patient experiences and unmet needs through online conversations, companies can design medications that better address patient concerns.

The future of sentiment analysis in pharma is bright. By embracing these advancements and integrating them into strategies, pharmaceutical companies can foster stronger relationships with patients, develop more effective medications, and contribute to improved healthcare outcomes.

CHAPTER

10

Emerging Trends and Advancements in Sentiment Analysis

Sentiment analysis has become a game-changer in many industries, and pharmaceuticals are no exception. But the field is constantly evolving. This chapter dives into the exciting new trends and advancements that will shape the future of sentiment analysis in pharma.

Getting Even Smarter: AI and NLP Take the Lead

- **Beyond Basic Sentiment**: Current sentiment analysis tools categorize data as positive, negative, or neutral. The future holds promise for more nuanced analysis. Advancements in Natural Language Processing (NLP) and Artificial Intelligence (AI) will allow tools to capture:
  - **Sarcasm**: Identifying and understanding sarcastic remarks hidden within online conversations.
  - **Sentiment Intensity**: Not all positive or negative sentiment is created equal. AI will help distinguish between mildly satisfied and highly enthusiastic patients.
  - **Emotions Beyond Basic Categories**: Going beyond basic emotions like happy or sad, future tools might detect anger, frustration, or fear within patient comments.

Breaking Down Dat Silos: A Holistic View

- **Integration with Other Data Sources**: Imagine combining sentiment analysis of social media conversations with real-world data like prescription trends or healthcare claims data. This integrated approach will provide a more comprehensive picture of patient experiences and treatment outcomes.
  - **Example**: Sentiment analysis reveals anxiety about the side effects of a new medicaiton. Combining this data with prescription trends might show a decrease in refills, suggesting patients might be abandoning treatment due to those anxieties.

Seeing Around the Corner: Predictive Analytics

- **From Reactive to Proactive**: Sentiment analysis isn't just about understanding the present. The future lies in prediction. By analyzing historical data and current trends, these advanced tools might be able to:
  - **Forecast Patient Concerns**: Proactively identify potential areas of future concern among patients based on online conversations.
  - **Public Perception for Drug Launches**: Analyze sentiment surrounding upcoming drug launches, allowing companies to address potential public perception issues before they escalate.

Real-Time Risk Management for Patient Safety

- **Early Warming System for Safety Concerns**: Sentiment analysis can be a powerful tool for real-time risk management. Companies can quickly identify potential safety concerns or adverse event reports by continuously monitoring online conversations. This allows for quicker intervention and improved patient safety.

The Rise of Empowered Patient: Communication Gets Personal

- **Patient-Centric Communication Strategies**: The future of healthcare is about empowering patients. Sentiment analysis can inform the development of personalized communication approaches:
  - **Example**: A company can identify patients with specific questions or concerns based on online reviews and tailor educational materials or FAQ sections on their website to address those needs directly.

These advancements promise a new era in pharma, characterized by:

- **Stronger Patient Relationships**: By understanding and addressing patient needs effectively, companies can build stronger, more trusting relationships.
- **Development of More Effective Medications**: Real-world data from sentiment analysis can inform drug development efforts, leading to medications that better address patient concerns and improve treatment outcomes.
- **Data-Driven Decision-Making**: Sentiment analysis empowers companies to make strategic decisions based on concrete data and patient insights, not just assumptions.

The future of sentiment analysis in pharmaceuticals is brimming with possibilities. By embracing these emerging trends and advancements, pharmaceutical companies can position themselves for success in a patient-centric, data-driven healthcare future.

10.1 The Role of Artificial Intelligence (AI) and Natural Language Processing (NLP) in Sentiment Analysis

Sentiment analysis is crucial in the pharmaceutical industry, helping companies understand patient perceptions of medications, brands, and treatments. However, this process relies heavily on the combined power of Artificial Intelligence (AI) and Natural Language Processing (NLP). Here's a deeper dive into their roles:

Natural Language Processing (NLP): Decoding the Language Puzzle

NLP acts as the foundation for sentiment analysis, providing the tools to understand the complexities of human language. Here's how it works in the context of pharma:

- **Grammar and Syntax**: Imagine analyzing a patient review that reads, "The medication didn't help my symptoms at all." NLP helps identify the negation (didn't) to accurately classify the sentiment as negative, even though positive words like "help" are present.
- **Vocabulary and Semantics**: Understanding the nuances of words is crucial. NLP can differentiate between "effective" (positive – successful treatment) and "efficacious" (neutral – describes the drug's potential to work), ensuring accurate sentiment classification.
    - **Example**: A social media post mentions a medication's "strong" side effects. NLP can recognize that "strong" can be negative in this context despite having a positive connotation in other situations (strong bond).

Artificial Intelligence (AI): The Learning Engine

Building on the foundation of NLP, AI takes sentiment analysis to the next level. Here's how AI tackles the task in the world of pharmaceuticals:

- **Identifying Sentiment**: AI algorithms are trained on massive datasets of labeled text data (positive, negative, neutral) related to pharmaceuticals. This training allows them to analyze new patient reviews and social media conversations, identifying patterns in language that indicate sentiment.
  - **Example**: An AI trained on medicaiton reviews can recognize phrases like "life-changing" or "miracle drug" as positive sentiment indicators, even though they are not explicitly positive words.
- **Capturing Emotion**: Advanced AI can delve deeper than basic positive/negative categories. For instance, analyzing a forum discussion about a medication's long wait times at pharmacies, AI might identify frustration or anxiety in patient comments, even if they don't use those exact words.
  - **Example**: A social media post reads, "Just started this medication, hope it works!" AI can not only identify the sentiment as hopeful (positive) but might also detect a hint of underlying anxiety due to using the word "hope."
- **Learning and Adapting**: The best AI keeps getting better! These algorithms are constantly learning from new data like patient reviews and social media trends. This allows them to adapt and improve their accuracy in sentiment analysis over time.
  - **Example**: As AI is explored to a wider range of patient experiences, it can learn to differentiate between genuine negative side effects and sarcastic remarks about medication side effects (e.g., "This medication is a miracle cure...for insomnia!").

Benefits of AI and NLP in Pharma

By working together, AI and NLP empower sentiment analysis in the pharmaceutical industry to go beyond basic positive/negative categorizations. This leads to several advantages:

- **More Accurate Insights**: AI and NLP provide a deeper understanding of patient sentiment, reducing the risk of misinterpreting reviews or social media conversations.
- **Unveiling Hidden Emotions**: Advanced AI can detect a wider range of emotions beyond basic categories, allowing companies to identify concerns or anxieties patients might not explicitly express.
- **Actionable Strategies**: By understanding the "why" behind patient sentiment (e.g., frustration with side effects, confusion about dosage), companies can develop targeted solutions and improve communication strategies.

In conclusion, AI and NLP are the driving forces behind powerful sentiment analysis in the pharmaceutical industry. By deciphering the complexities of human language and identifying the emotions underlying patient communications, AI and NLP empower companies to make data-driven decisions, improve patient care, and build stronger brand loyalty.

10.2 Exploring Advanced Sentiment Analysis Techniques Like Aspect-Based Sentiment Analysis

While traditional sentiment analysis offers a basic understanding of overall opinion (positive, negative, neutral), the pharmaceutical industry can delve deeper with advanced techniques. Here's how these techniques unlock richer patient insights:

1. **Aspect-Based Sentiment Analysis: A Microscopic Look**
   - Imagine a patient review for a new cholesterol medication: "This medication **lowers my cholesterol** (positive), but the **side effects are terrible** (negative) – constant headaches!" Traditional sentiment analysis might classify it as negative. However, aspect-based sentiment analysis offers a more detailed picture:
     - **Identifying Aspects**: The technique first recognizes the different aspects (features) discussed. In this case, the aspects are "effectiveness" (lowering cholesterol) and "side effects" (headaches).
     - **Sentiment Classification**: Once aspects are identified, sentiment analysis is applied individually. This review reveals a positive sentiment toward effectiveness but a negative sentiment toward side effects.

   Benefits in Pharma:

   - **Targeted Improvements**: It will be easier to identify areas for improvement. Negative sentiment toward side effects might prompt research into solutions to mitigate them.
   - **Effective Communication Strategies**: Knowing which aspects generate positive or negative sentiment allows companies to tailor communication. For example, they can highlight the medication's effectiveness while addressing concerns about side effects in marketing materials and patient education resources.

- **Example**: Social media discussions about a new diabetes medicaiton might reveal positive sentiment towards its ease of use but negative sentiment towards its high cost. This insight can inform pricing strategies or the development of patient assistance programs.

2. **Opinion Spam Detection: Sifting Through the Noise**
   - Not all online reviews are genuine. Spam detection techniques help identify fake reviews or biased opinions that might skew sentiment analysis results.
     - **Example**: A competitor might launch a campaign posting negative reviews about a medication's effectiveness. Opinion spam detection can help identify these fake reviews and ensure accurate sentiment analysis reflects genuine patient experiences.
3. **Sentiment Intensity Analysis**
   - Not all positive or negative sentiments are created equal. Sentiment intensity analysis goes beyond basic categories and measures the strength of the sentiment expressed.
     - **Example**: A patient review might say, "This medication slightly (low intensity) helped my symptoms, but I am still looking for a better solution." This reveals a less enthusiastic positive sentiment than a review that says, "This medication is a miracle cure (high intensity) for my condition!" Understanding intensity allows companies to prioritize areas for improvement.
4. **Emotion Detection: Uncovering the "Why" Behind" Opinions**
   - Advanced sentiment analysis can identify specific emotions beyond basic categories.
     - **Example**: A forum discussion about a medication's complex dosing schedule might reveal not just negative sentiments but also feelings of frustration or anxiety

among patients. This can inform the development of simpler dosing instructions or educational materials to address patient anxieties.

The Future of Advanced Sentiment Analysis

By incorporating these techniques, pharmaceutical companies can move beyond basic sentiment and gain a nuanced understanding of patient experiences. This empowers them to:

- **Develop More Effective Medications**: By understanding specific patient concerns (e.g., side effects), companies can tailor drug development efforts to address those needs.
- **Improve Patient Communication**: Knowing what aspects of medications generate strong emotions allows for more targeted communication strategies, fostering trust and stronger patient relationships.
- **Contribute to Better Healthcare Outcomes**: Deeper patient insights can inform the development of educational materials and support programs, improving patient care and medication adherence.

The future of sentiment analysis in pharmaceuticals is full of possibilities. By leveraging advanced techniques, companies can unlock a deeper understanding of the patient voice, leading to a more patient-centric and successful future in healthcare.

10.3 The Future of Sentiment Analysis and Its Impact on the Pharmaceutical Industry

The future of sentiment analysis in the pharmaceutical industry has exciting possibilities. Here's a glimpse into what's on the horizon and how it will revolutionize the way pharmaceutical companies operate:

1. **Advanced AI and NLP Techniques**:
    - **Beyond Basic Sentiment**: Current sentiment analysis tools categorize data as positive, negative, or neutral. The future holds promise for more sophisticated AI and NLP (Natural Language Processing) techniques that can capture:
        - **Sarcasm**: Identifying and understanding the meaning behind sarcastic remarks hidden in online conversations.
        - **Sentiment Intensity**: Not all positive or negative sentiments are created equal. AI will help distinguish between mildly satisfied and highly enthusiastic patients.
        - **A Wider Range of Emotions**: Future tools might detect anger, frustration, or fear in patient comments, going beyond basic emotions like happiness or sadness.
2. **Holistic View with Integrated Data Sources**:
    - **Breaking Down Data Silos**: Sentiment analysis won't exist in isolation. Imagine combining it with real-world data like prescription trends, healthcare claims data, and clinical trial results. This holistic view will provide a more comprehensive picture of patient experiences and treatment outcomes.
        - **Example**: Sentiment analysis reveals anxiety about the side effects of a new medication. Combining this data with prescription trends showing a decrease in refills might suggest patients are abandoning treatment due to those anxieties.

3. **Predictive Analytics: Proactive Problem-Solving**:
   - **From Reactive to Proactive**: Sentiment analysis isn't just about understanding the present. By analyzing historical data and current trends, these advanced tools might be able to:
     - **Forecast Patient Concerns**: Proactively identify potential areas of future concern among patients based on online conversations.
     - **Public Perception for Drug Launches**: Analyze sentiment surrounding upcoming drug launches, allowing companies to address potential public perception issues before they escalate.
4. **Real-Time Risk Management for Patient Safety**:
   - **Early Warning System for Safety Concerns**: Sentiment analysis can be a powerful tool for real-time risk management. Companies can quickly identify potential safety concerns or adverse event reports by constantly monitoring online conversations. This allows for quicker intervention and improved patient safety.
5. **The Rise of the Empowered Patient: Communication Gets Personal**
   - **Patient-Centric Communication Strategies**: The future of healthcare is about empowering patients. Sentiment analysis can inform the development of personalized communication approaches.
     - **Example**: A company can identify patients with specific questions or concerns based on online reviews and tailor educational materials or FAQ sections on their website to address those needs directly.

Impact on the Pharmaceutical Industry

These advancements will usher in a new era in pharma, characterized by:

- **Stronger Patient Relationships:** By understanding and addressing patient needs effectively, companies can build stronger, more trusting relationships.
- **Development of More Effective Medications**: Real-world data from sentiment analysis can inform drug development efforts, leading to medications that better address patient concerns and improve treatment outcomes.
- **Data-Driven Decision Making**: Sentiment analysis empowers companies to make strategic decisions based on concrete data and patient insights, not just assumptions.

Overall, the future of sentiment analysis in pharmaceuticals is one of continuous improvement and deeper understanding. By embracing these advancements, pharmaceutical companies can position themselves for success in a patient-centric, data-driven healthcare future.

CHAPTER

11

Conclusion: The Power of Listening in Pharma Marketing

1. **The Power of Listening in Pharma Marketing: Unveiling Patient Insights Through Sentiment Analysis**
   - In today's world, the patient's voice is more important than ever. Pharmaceutical companies can no longer afford to operate in silos, developing medications without a deep understanding of the needs and concerns of the people who will be using them. Sentiment analysis offers a powerful tool for pharma marketing, allowing companies to listen to patient conversations and glean valuable insights that can inform everything from product development to marketing strategies.
2. **The Transformative Power of Sentiment Analysis**
   - Sentiment analysis is a game-changer for the pharmaceutical industry. Companies can understand patients' feelings about their medications, brands, and treatment options by analyzing online reviews, social media conversations, and other text data. This goldmine of patient insights can be used to identify areas for improvement, develop more effective communication strategies, and improve patient care.
3. **Key Benefits of Sentiment Analysis for Pharma Marketing**
   - Sentiment analysis has numerous benefits for pharmaceutical marketing. By listening to patients,

companies can build a stronger brand reputation, improve the patient experience, develop targeted communication strategies, and make data-driven decisions that lead to better outcomes.

4. **The Future of Sentiment Analysis in Pharma**
   - The future of sentiment analysis in pharma is bright. As AI and NLP evolve, sentiment analysis tools will become even more sophisticated, capable of capturing the nuances of human language and identifying a wider range of emotions. By integrating sentiment analysis with other data sources and leveraging predictive analytics, companies can better understand patient experiences and proactively address their needs. Real-time risk management will ensure patient safety, while patient-centric communications will foster trust and empower patients to take an active role in their healthcare.

In conclusion, sentiment analysis is a transformative tool for pharmaceutical marketing. By listening to patients and understanding their needs and concerns, companies can develop better products, improve communication, and build stronger relationships with the people they serve. As sentiment analysis continues to evolve, the possibilities for improving patient care and health outcomes are limitless. Embrace the power of listening and unlock the true potential of pharmaceutical marketing.

11.1 The Importance of Integrating Sentiment Analysis of Your Overall Marketing Strategy

In today's digital age, customers are constantly voicing their opinions online. Sentiment analysis is a powerful tool to help you listen to these conversations and understand how people feel about your brand, medications, or treatments. But why integrate sentiment analysis into your overall marketing strategy? Consider the following reasons:

1. **Deeper Customer Understanding**:
   - Traditional marketing research might rely on surveys or focus groups, which can be limited in scope and may not capture the full range of customer sentiment.
   - Sentiment analysis harnesses vast online data, including social media posts, reviews, and forum discussions. It allows you to better understand customer experiences, concerns, and preferences.
2. **Identify Areas for Improvement**:
   - Understanding what people are saying, you can pinpoint areas where your brand or medications might fall short.
   - For example, sentiment analysis might reveal that patients struggle with a medication's side effects. This valuable insight can inform marketing efforts to address those concerns or spark product development efforts to improve the medication.
3. **Develop Targeted Communication**:
   - Not all customers are the same. Sentiment analysis can help you segment your audience based on their needs and concerns.
   - This allows you to develop targeted marketing messages that resonate with specific patient groups.
     - **Example**: Sentiment analysis might reveal a group of patients anxious about a medication's long-term effects.

You can then develop marketing materials addressing those anxieties and providing educational resources.

4. **Build Brand Trust and Reputation**:
   - You build trust and credibility by actively listening to your customers and addressing their concerns.
   - Sentiment analysis allows you to demonstrate that you care about patient experiences and are committed to improvement. This can increase brand loyalty and promote positive word-of-mouth marketing.
5. **Data-Driven Decision Making**:
   - Marketing decisions should not be based on guesswork. Sentiment analysis provides valuable data and insights that can inform your marketing strategy.
   - You can track sentiment over time, measure the effectiveness of marketing campaigns, and identify areas for optimization.

Integrating sentiment analysis is not just about understanding overall positive or negative feedback; it's about gaining a nuanced view of customer sentiment. By incorporating this tool into your marketing strategy, you can:

- Develop more effective marketing campaigns
- Improve patient experiences
- Build stronger brand relationships
- Ultimately achieve greater success in the competitive pharmaceutical marketplace.

11.2 The Evolving Role of Pharma Brand Managers in the Age of Big Data and Customer Insights

The world of pharmaceuticals is undergoing a digital revolution, and the role of the brand manager is evolving. Big data and the explosion of customer insights are transforming how pharma companies connect with patients and healthcare providers. Here's a breakdown of how pharma brand managers are adapting to this new age:

From Broadcast to Dialogue: The Rise of Patient-Centric Marketing

- Traditionally, pharmaceutical marketing relied on a broadcast model, pushing messages about medication through one-way channels such as television ads or doctor visits.
- In the age of big data, the focus has shifted to a two-way dialogue. Brand managers leverage customer insights to understand patient needs, concerns, and preferences. This allows them to develop targeted communication that resonates with specific patient groups.

Shifting Skills: From Product Experts to Data Analyzers

- In the past, brand managers excelled at product knowledge and crafting messages.
- Today's successful brand manager needs to be data-savvy. They must understand how to interpret sentiment analysis reports, identify trends in customer conversations, and translate those insights into actionable marketing strategies.

Embracing New Tools and Technologies

- Big data and customer insights are complex. Brand managers are increasingly utilizing new technologies like:
- **Sentiment analysis tools**: To understand the emotional tone of online conversations about medications and brands.

- **Social media listening platforms**: To track mentions of brands and medications online and identify emerging trends.
- **Customer Relationship Management (CRM) Systems**: To manage patient interactions and personalize marketing efforts.

Collaboration is Key: Partnering with Data Scientists and Market Researchers

- The vast amount of data can be overwhelming. Brand managers are forging stronger relationships with data scientists and market researchers to extract meaningful insights and translate them into actionable marketing strategies.

Focus on Value: Demonstrating ROI in a Data-Driven World

- Measuring the return on investment (ROI) of marketing campaigns is crucial. Brand managers must demonstrate how their data-driven strategies impact patient outcomes, brand awareness, and medication sales.

The Future of Pharma Brand Management

The future of pharma brand management is all about harnessing the power of big data and customer insights to create targeted, patient-centric marketing campaigns. Successful brand managers will be:

- **Data-driven decision makers**: Adept at analyzing and translating data into actionable insights.
- **Storytellers**: Communicating complex information about medications compellingly for patients and healthcare providers.
- **Tech-savvy collaborators**: Working effectively with data scientists, market researchers, and other stakeholders to leverage the power of big data.
- **Patient Advocates**: Understanding and championing the needs and concerns of patients in all marketing efforts.

By embracing these changes, pharma brand managers can play a pivotal role in healthcare marketing, ensuring that medications reach the patients who need them most and that marketing messages are relevant, informative, and effective.

11.3 Final Thoughts and the Future of Customer Centricity in Pharma

The pharmaceutical industry is at a crossroads. For decades, the focus was on products and sales with less emphasis on the "customer" — the patients and healthcare providers (HCPs) who rely on these medications. However, the tide is turning. Customer centricity is no longer a fad; it's the key to success in a competitive and evolving healthcare landscape.

Key Takeaways of Customer Centricity in Pharma

- **Shifting Focus**: The focus has moved from medications to the patient journey and HCP experience. Understanding their needs, concerns, and decision-making processes is crucial.
- **The Power of Data**: Big data and customer insights are transforming marketing strategies. Sentiment analysis, social media listening, and CRM systems empower companies to tailor communication and develop targeted campaigns.
- **Building Trust**: Patient trust is paramount. Customer centricity fosters transparency, open communication, and a commitment to addressing patient concerns. This leads to stronger brand loyalty and advocacy.
- **Collaboration is Key**: Breaking down silos within pharma companies is essential. Brand managers, data scientists, market researchers, and product development teams must work together to leverage customer insights effectively.
- **The Rise of the Empowered Patient**: Patients are taking a more active role in their healthcare. Pharma companies must cater to this shift by providing educational resources, addressing patient anxieties, and fostering two-way communication.

The Future of Customer Centricity in Pharma

The future of customer-centricity in pharma is bright, fueled by advancements in technology and a growing patient voice:

- **Advanced AI and NLP**: These tools will enable an even deeper understanding of patient sentiment, identifying subtle emotions and tailoring communication accordingly.
- **Real-Time Risk Management**: Sentiment analysis can monitor real-time online conversations, allowing for faster identification and mitigation of potential medication risks.
- **Personalized Medicine**: Customer insights can inform the development of personalized treatment plans and medications that cater to individual patient needs and preferences.
- **Omnichannel Communication**: Patients expect seamless communication across all platforms. Pharmacy companies must develop omnichannel strategies that provide consistent, relevant information across all touchpoints.
- **Focus on Patient Outcomes**: The ultimate goal is to improve patient health outcomes. Customer centricity will drive a focus on medication adherence, disease management, and overall patient well-being.

Conclusion

By embracing customer-centricity, pharmaceutical companies can strengthen their relationships with patients and HCPs, develop more effective medications, and contribute to a healthier future for all. In the age of big data and empowered patients, those prioritizing the "customer" will be the pharmaceutical industry leaders tomorrow.

Epilogue: A Future of Listening

Five years after Sarah's initial search, the pharmaceutical industry landscape metamorphosed. Sentiment analysis has become a cornerstone of patient-centric drug development. Pharma companies were no longer operating in the dark; they were actively listening to the online chorus of patient voices.

Sarah herself had become a patient advocate, her story a testament to the power of online communities. The medication she'd researched had proven effective for her, and she now used her experience to help others navigate the complexities of the healthcare system.

The Evolution of Listening:

Sentiment analysis had matured beyond basic positive/negative categorization. Advanced techniques were now delving into the "why" behind patient sentiment, uncovering anxieties, frustrations, and unmet needs. This deeper understanding was informing product development in groundbreaking ways.

Medications were being tailored to address specific patient concerns. Dosage forms and delivery methods were optimized based on real-world feedback. Side effects were being proactively mitigated through early identification of patient anxieties.

The Power of Collaboration:

The walls between pharmaceutical companies, patients, and healthcare providers had begun to crumble. Online communities fostered open communication, allowing patients to share experiences, ask questions, and provide direct feedback to researchers and developers.

A New Era of Trust:

This transparency fostered trust, a critical ingredient in the patient-physician relationship. Patients felt heard and understood, leading to better medication adherence and improved health outcomes.

The Road Ahead:

The journey, however, was far from over. Artificial intelligence and natural language processing were poised to revolutionize sentiment analysis further. The ability to detect emotions beyond basic sentiment and even predict patient behavior based on online conversations held immense potential.

The Call to Action:

The book concludes with a call to action. The power of sentiment analysis lies in the technology and the commitment to listen and act on the insights it reveals. As we move forward, the question remains:

Are you ready to truly listen to the voices that matter most?

The future of healthcare hinges on the answer.

Glossary

- **Sentiment Analysis:** The process of computationally identifying and classifying the emotional tone (positive, negative, or neutral) within a piece of text data.
- **Natural Language Processing (NLP):** A subfield of Artificial Intelligence (AI) concerned with the interaction between computers and human language. NLP techniques are crucial for sentiment analysis, enabling computers to understand the nuances of human language.
- **Machine Learning (ML):** A field of AI focused on algorithms that can learn from data without explicit programming. Sentiment analysis models are often built using machine learning techniques.
- **Lexicon-Based Analysis:** A method that relies on pre-defined lists of words with positive, negative, or neutral sentiment associations. The presence and frequency of these words determine the sentiment of a text.
- **Machine Learning-Based Analysis:** A more sophisticated approach that uses machine learning algorithms trained on massive datasets of labeled text data (positive, negative, neutral). These algorithms can identify sentiment patterns and even classify emotions beyond basic categories.
- **Aspect-Based Sentiment Analysis:** An advanced technique that goes beyond overall sentiment and identifies the sentiment towards specific aspects (features) of a product, service, or

topic. For example, analyzing medication reviews might reveal positive sentiment toward its effectiveness but negative sentiment toward side effects.

- **Opinion Spam Detection:** Techniques used to identify fake reviews, biased opinions, or marketing messages disguised as genuine customer reviews. These techniques help ensure the accuracy of sentiment analysis results.
- **Sentiment Intensity Analysis:** Not all positive or negative sentiment is created equal. This technique goes beyond basic categories and measures the strength of the sentiment expressed (e.g., slightly satisfied vs. extremely frustrated).
- **Emotion Detection:** Advanced sentiment analysis can identify specific emotions beyond basic categories like happy or sad. This can help understand the "why" behind an opinion (e.g., frustration with medication dosing instructions).
- **Text Analytics:** The broader field encompassing various techniques for analyzing and extracting information from textual data. Sentiment analysis is a specific type of text analytics focused on understanding emotional tone.

Further Resources on Sentiment Analysis Tools and Techniques

Online Resources:

- **MonkeyLearn:** A company offering a user-friendly sentiment analysis platform with tutorials and resources:
- **Google Cloud Natural Language API:** Documentation and guides on Google's sentiment analysis service: https://cloud.google.com/natural-language/docs/analyzing-sentiment
- **Amazon Comprehend** Information on Amazon's sentiment analysis service within their Comprehend suite: https://docs.aws.amazon.com/comprehend/latest/dg/how-sentiment.html.
- **Stanford CoreNLP:** A popular open-source NLP toolkit with sentiment analysis capabilities: https://stanfordnlp.github.io/CoreNLP/
- **National Institute of Standards and Technology (NIST) Sentiment Analysis Evaluation (SEMEVAL):** A benchmark for evaluating sentiment analysis tools, offering insights into the strengths and weaknesses of different approaches: https://pages.nist.gov/trojai/docs/nlp-sentiment-classification-apr2021.html

Articles and Research Papers:

- **"A Survey on Opinion Mining and Sentiment Analysis" by Pang, B. and Lee, L.:** A comprehensive research paper exploring various sentiment analysis techniques: https://dl.acm.org/doi/abs/10.1561/1500000011
- **"Aspect-Based Sentiment Analysis with Latent Dirichlet Allocation" by Hu, M. and Liu, B.:** A research paper delving into aspect-based sentiment analysis: https://dl.acm.org/doi/abs/10.4018/JCIT.20220701.oa3

Books:

- **"Sentiment Analysis for Social Media" by Mike Thelwall:** A practical guide to sentiment analysis for social media data.
- **"Text Mining with R" by Julia Silge and David Robinson:** A book exploring text mining techniques, including sentiment analysis, using the R programming language.
- **"Sentiment Analysis: From Opinion Mining to Emotion Sensing" by Bing Liu:** A comprehensive textbook on sentiment analysis, covering theory, techniques, and applications.

Additionally:

- Consider attending industry conferences or webinars related to NLP and sentiment analysis. These events offer opportunities to learn from experts and network with professionals in the field.
- Many universities offer online courses or lectures on sentiment analysis. These can provide a structured learning experience.

About the Author

Subba Rao Chaganti has a master's in business administration and over fifty-two years of pharmaceutical marketing experience. His experience covers all marketing facets, from sales management to product management to heading the total marketing activity. He has experience in domestic and international marketing and the Indian and multinational sectors.

For a few years, he taught a course on advertising and brand management at the GITAM Institute of Foreign Trade (now part of the GITAM University) at Visakhapatnam and a course on international marketing at Jawaharlal Nehru Technological University (JNTU) at Hyderabad in India as a visiting faculty.

He lives in Farmington, Connecticut, USA, and can be reached at subbarao.chaganti@gmail.com.

Here is a list of his published books:

1. Pharmaceutical Marketing in India: Concepts, Strategy, Cases
2. Game Plans for Post-Gatt Era: Action Agenda of the Indian Pharmaceutical Industry
3. Compete or Forfeit! Strategies for Sustainable Competitive Edge in Pharma Product Patent Era
4. Pharmaceutical Marketing in India for Today and Tomorrow, 25th Anniversary Edition

5. Bullseyes and Blunders: Lessons from 100 Cases in Pharmaceutical Marketing
6. Digital Pharma Marketing Playbook: Winning with the New Rules of Engagement
7. Cracking the Generics Code: Your Single-Source Success Manual for Multi-Source Products
8. Reimagine Pharma Marketing: Make it Future-Proof!
9. Brand Positioning in Pharma
10. Transactional to Transformational Marketing in Pharma: The Science of *Why* and the Art of *How*
11. A to Z of Pharmaceutical Marketing: World's First and Only Encylopedia, Set of 2 Volumes
12. The Synergy of Minds: Human+AI Orchestrating the Pharma Marketing Revolution
13. Design Thinking for Pharma: Forget Features, Focus on Feelings
14. The Pharma Product Manager: Handbook for Navigating the Digital Frontier

www.ingramcontent.com/pod-product-compliance
Ingram Content Group UK Ltd.
Pitfield, Milton Keynes, MK11 3LW, UK
UKHW021951270726
14060UKWH00002B/461